BILL GRANGER

EVERY DAY

PHOTOGRAPHY BY PETRINA TINSLAY

MURDOCH BOOKS

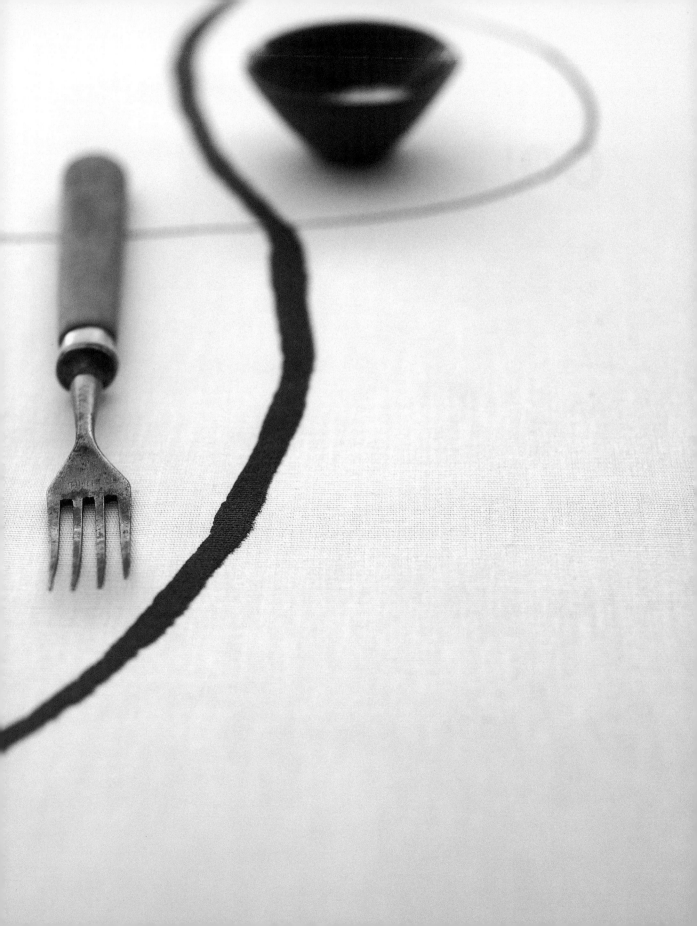

CONTENTS

006   MONDAY

energizing breakfasts; glam salads; spa food

038   TUESDAY

start the day; packed lunches; easy weekday dinners

076   WEDNESDAY

quick breakfasts; not-your-everyday sandwiches; after-school
milk and cookies; easy weekday dinners

114   THURSDAY

breakfast on the run; kids' meals; friends for dinner

148   FRIDAY

hangover breakfasts; friday drinks; "come over for a chop!"

178   SATURDAY

relaxed breakfasts; fishmarket lunch; baking; dinner parties

214   SUNDAY

big breakfasts; sunday roasts; soup suppers

"I come from a family of butchers and bakers so it's fair to say that food, in some shape or form, was always going to be my destiny. With three busy restaurants in Sydney, it's inevitable that food is often the first thing on my mind when I wake up in the morning and the last thing I think about at night, but it's also what gives my life rhythm. From healthy family breakfasts, to special Saturday-night dinners for friends, or seeing my three daughters' faces light up when I take a tray of cookies out of the oven, my week revolves around the endless pleasures of good food. And do you know what? I wouldn't have it any other way."

Early morning is my monday favourite time of day, always has been, and Monday has never been a problem for me. It's the warm-up for the week ahead and I like the sense of anticipation. I love waking up early and leaving the house before anyone else is even awake.

We're lucky because we live by the ocean and I can be on the beach in just a few minutes. I guess our amazing climate and beautiful morning light make it easy too, but even in winter when it's dark and chilly I get up early. Ideally, I'd love to get up at 5.30 every morning — a thought that just horrifies Natalie! I like nothing better than pottering in the kitchen while it's still dark outside... there's something very comforting and nurturing about it. I love to start the week on a positive note — grab it and take control. Whatever the time of year I can walk, run or swim, clear my head and get organized for the day ahead. What's that old saying? That the man who is up early owns the world? It's so true.

Monday is everybody's day for good intentions, judging by the number of people I see jogging and walking on Bondi Beach at 6.30 am. It's the day that you can never get a spot at the gym, everybody is out power walking, the parks are busy... it's like a New Year's resolution every Monday. That's one of the things I love about Sydney: the people are energetic and alive — there's something really wonderful, and very sociable, about it.

I try to take that with me when I travel. If I'm in London or Chicago or wherever, I will go for a walk in the park in the morning. Even on a misty, dark and cold November morning, Hyde Park is one of the most beautiful places.

So Monday is my day for clearing my head and roughly planning the meals for the week ahead. I try to eat healthily a few nights a week, to balance out the weekend's indulgences. And, just like everyone else, when I'm tired or worn out I love to take comfort in food — I find it very easy to overeat!

I'm always amazed at people who don't eat breakfast. I love breakfasts — maybe that's why my restaurants have become well-known for them. As far as I can see, if you eat a good breakfast you've done a third of your day's work for eating well. It's pretty simple logic. Healthy eating isn't about denying yourself, it's about eating. I can't bear talk about counting calories — it should be about the quality of ingredients and what you're putting into your body.

Being a restaurateur, I see a lot of people who have a complex relationship with food and, as the father of three young girls, I don't want to encourage that. I want them to have a really healthy attitude to food and to be happy about themselves; to see food as one of life's great pleasures. There's nothing wrong with an occasional chocolate bar or an ice cream after school if you're having a healthy dinner every night. It's just commonsense to me.

ENERGIZING BREAKFASTS

APPLE, DRIED CHERRY AND ALMOND LOAF

MAKES 12 SLICES

50 G (1³/₄ OZ/¹/₂ CUP) ROLLED OATS
300 ML (10¹/₂ FL OZ) MILK
240 G (9 OZ/2 CUPS) SELF-RAISING FLOUR (YOU CAN USE WHOLEMEAL)
1 TEASPOON BAKING POWDER
125 G (4¹/₂ OZ) DRIED CHERRIES
50 G (1³/₄ OZ) DRIED APPLE, DICED
75 G (2³/₄ OZ/¹/₃ CUP) SOFT BROWN SUGAR
1 TEASPOON GROUND CINNAMON
3 TABLESPOONS HONEY
1 EGG, LIGHTLY BEATEN
3 TABLESPOONS ROUGHLY CHOPPED ALMONDS, PLUS 2 TABLESPOONS EXTRA

TO SERVE
FRESH RICOTTA AND HONEY

Put the oats in a bowl, pour the milk over them and leave to soak for 30 minutes. Preheat the oven to 180°C (350°F/Gas 4). Lightly grease and line a 1 kg (2 lb 4 oz) loaf tin with baking paper.

Sift the flour and baking powder into a bowl and stir in the rolled oats, dried fruit, sugar, cinnamon, honey, egg and almonds. Mix together well.

Spoon the mixture into the tin, level the top and sprinkle with the extra almonds. Bake the loaf for 45 minutes, or until it is golden brown on top and cooked through. Leave it to cool a little in the tin before turning out onto a wire rack to cool completely. Toast and serve with ricotta and honey.

"Don't worry, I don't bake on a Monday morning! I make this in advance to toast for a quick breakfast."

BERRY HOTCAKES

MAKES 12

165 G (5¾ OZ) FROZEN MIXED BERRIES, THAWED
3 TABLESPOONS CASTER (SUPERFINE) SUGAR
90 G (3¼ OZ/¾ CUP) PLAIN (ALL-PURPOSE) FLOUR
90 G (3¼ OZ) WHOLEMEAL FLOUR
1¼ TEASPOONS BAKING POWDER
PINCH OF SALT
3 EGGS, SEPARATED
250 ML (9 FL OZ/1 CUP) SKIM MILK
125 G (4½ OZ/½ CUP) FRESH RICOTTA
A LITTLE MELTED BUTTER, FOR FRYING

TO SERVE
MAPLE SYRUP

Preheat the oven to 120°C (235°F/Gas ½). Lightly mash the berries with a tablespoon of the sugar.

Sift the flours, baking powder and salt into a large mixing bowl and add the remaining sugar. In a separate bowl, whisk together the egg yolks and milk. Make a well in the centre of the dry ingredients and stir in the egg mixture until just combined. Gently stir in the ricotta.

Beat the egg whites until stiff peaks form. Carefully fold into the batter until just combined. Fold in the berries in two or three strokes to give a marbled effect — do not overmix.

Heat a large frying pan over medium-high heat and brush with a little melted butter. For each hotcake, drop ⅓ cup of the batter into the pan. Cook for 2 minutes, or until bubbles appear on the surface. Turn and cook the other side for 1 minute, then tip out onto a plate and keep warm in the oven while you cook the rest. Serve with maple syrup.

HEALTHY TOAST TOPPINGS

EACH SERVES 2

TAHINI AND TOMATO
Spread your toast with 2 tablespoons of unhulled tahini and top with slices of ripe tomato. Season with sea salt and garnish with torn flat-leaf (Italian) parsley. Serve immediately. Tahini is a sesame paste you can buy in health food shops and most supermarkets.

GRAVLAX AND CREAM CHEESE
Spread 2 tablespoons of light cream cheese over toast and top with a slice of gravlax or smoked salmon. Scatter with a little finely sliced red onion and 1 teaspoon of rinsed capers. Squeeze lemon juice over the top and serve immediately.

GLAM SALADS

SPICY SQUID SALAD WITH CUCUMBER AND CAPERS

SERVES 4

1 KG (2 LB 4 OZ) SQUID, CLEANED, SCORED ON THE INSIDE AND CUT INTO STRIPS
2½ TABLESPOONS OLIVE OIL
2 GARLIC CLOVES, CRUSHED
1 LONG RED CHILLI, SEEDED AND FINELY CHOPPED
1 LEBANESE (SHORT) CUCUMBER, PEELED, HALVED, SEEDED AND CUT INTO SMALL HALF-MOONS
200 G (7 OZ) YELLOW TEARDROP TOMATOES, HALVED
2 CELERY STALKS, THINLY SLICED ON THE DIAGONAL
SMALL HANDFUL CELERY LEAVES
LARGE HANDFUL FRESH BASIL LEAVES
1 TABLESPOON LEMON JUICE
SEA SALT
FRESHLY GROUND BLACK PEPPER
1 TABLESPOON SALTED BABY CAPERS, RINSED

Put the squid in a non-metallic bowl with 1½ tablespoons of the olive oil, the garlic and chilli and stir well to coat the squid. Cover and leave in the fridge to marinate for 2–3 hours.

Heat a large frying pan over high heat. Add the squid and cook for 1–2 minutes on each side until it is just cooked — take care not to overcook the squid or it will be tough.

Put the cucumber, tomatoes, celery, celery leaves and basil in a large bowl. Whisk together the remaining olive oil and lemon juice and season with sea salt and freshly ground black pepper. Add the squid to the bowl and toss well. Pile the salad onto a large platter, sprinkle with the capers and drizzle the lemon dressing over the top. Serve immediately.

"Make sure you don't overcook the squid — you don't want rubber bands!"

PEA, FETA AND MINT SALAD

SERVES 4

200 G (7 OZ) FRESH PEAS
3 TABLESPOONS OLIVE OIL
1 ONION, FINELY DICED
2 TEASPOONS DIJON MUSTARD
1 TABLESPOON RED WINE VINEGAR
1 TABLESPOON HONEY
SEA SALT
FRESHLY GROUND BLACK PEPPER
35 G (1¼ OZ) SHELLED PISTACHIO NUTS, ROUGHLY CHOPPED
LARGE HANDFUL FRESH MINT LEAVES
50 G (1¾ OZ) SNOW PEA (MANGETOUT) LEAVES OR BABY ENGLISH SPINACH
75 G (2¾ OZ) FETA CHEESE, CRUMBLED

Blanch the peas in boiling water for 2 minutes, or until they are just tender and bright green. Refresh immediately under cold water. Heat a small pan over medium heat. Add 1 tablespoon of the oil and cook the onion, stirring, for 5 minutes, or until it is soft.

Whisk together the mustard, remaining olive oil, vinegar and honey and season with salt and pepper.

Mix the onion, peas and pistachios in a salad bowl and pour the dressing over the top. Add the mint and snow pea leaves and gently toss through the salad. Sprinkle with feta to serve.

"Snow pea leaves aren't always easy to find, but this salad is worth the hunt. Baby English spinach is a worthy substitute."

PRAWN SALAD WITH COCONUT DRESSING

SERVES 4

350 G (12 OZ/2 BUNCHES) ASPARAGUS, SLICED ON THE DIAGONAL
750 G (1 LB 10 OZ) COOKED KING PRAWNS (SHRIMP), PEELED AND DEVEINED, TAILS INTACT
LARGE HANDFUL FRESH THAI BASIL LEAVES
LARGE HANDFUL FRESH CORIANDER (CILANTRO) LEAVES
COCONUT DRESSING, BELOW
2 FRESH MAKRUT (KAFFIR LIME) LEAVES, CENTRE VEINS REMOVED, THINLY SLICED

Blanch the asparagus in a saucepan of lightly salted boiling water for 1–2 minutes until it is bright green and crisply tender. Refresh under cold running water immediately and drain well.

Gently toss together the asparagus, prawns and herbs, then pile onto a serving platter and drizzle with the dressing. Sprinkle with the makrut leaves before serving.

COCONUT DRESSING

MAKES 125 ML (4 FL OZ/½ CUP)

½ TEASPOON RICE FLOUR
125 ML (4 FL OZ/½ CUP) COCONUT MILK
1 TEASPOON SUGAR
2 TEASPOONS FISH SAUCE
2 TEASPOONS LIME JUICE
1 SMALL RED CHILLI, SEEDED AND THINLY SLICED

Mix the rice flour with 1 tablespoon of the coconut milk. Heat the remaining coconut milk in a small saucepan. Stir in the rice flour mixture and cook until it has slightly thickened. Add the sugar, fish sauce, lime juice and chilli and cook for 1 minute.

"This versatile coconut dressing works brilliantly with poached chicken, too."

LENTIL, BEAN AND PARSLEY SALAD

SERVES 4

185 G (6½ OZ/1 CUP) PUY (SMALL BLUE/GREEN) LENTILS
2 TABLESPOONS EXTRA VIRGIN OLIVE OIL
1 TABLESPOON LEMON JUICE
2 TEASPOONS RED WINE VINEGAR
PINCH OF CASTER (SUPERFINE) SUGAR
SEA SALT
FRESHLY GROUND BLACK PEPPER
150 G (5½ OZ) SMALL GREEN BEANS, TOPPED
2 CELERY STALKS, JULIENNED
SMALL HANDFUL FRESH FLAT-LEAF (ITALIAN) PARSLEY LEAVES

Place the lentils in a saucepan with 750 ml (26 fl oz/3 cups) of water and bring to the boil. Reduce the heat and simmer for 15–20 minutes, or until tender, then drain. Whisk together the olive oil, lemon juice, vinegar, sugar, salt and pepper in a large bowl. Add the lentils and leave to cool.

Blanch the beans in a saucepan of boiling water until they are bright green and crisply tender. Rinse under cold running water and then drain well. Add the beans, celery and parsley to the lentils and toss together gently.

"Puy lentils have a wonderful bite but I sometimes use tinned organic Italian lentils to save time — just give them a quick rinse."

"Replace the turnip with fresh corn kernels, shaved from the cob, for a summery version."

SPA FOOD

VEGETABLE SOUP

SERVES 4

30 G (1 OZ) BUTTER
1 LARGE LEEK, WHITE PART ONLY, THINLY SLICED
2 CELERY STALKS, DICED
2 LARGE RED POTATOES, DICED
1 TURNIP, PEELED AND DICED
1.5 LITRES (52 FL OZ/6 CUPS) VEGETABLE STOCK
SEA SALT
FRESHLY GROUND BLACK PEPPER
90 G ($3\frac{1}{4}$ OZ/$\frac{1}{2}$ CUP) SMALL PASTA (SUCH AS MACARONI)
1 LARGE ZUCCHINI (COURGETTE), DICED
150 G ($5\frac{1}{2}$ OZ) GREEN BEANS, TOPPED AND CUT INTO SHORT LENGTHS
150 G ($5\frac{1}{2}$ OZ/1 CUP) FRESH PEAS

Melt the butter in a large saucepan over medium heat. Add the leek, celery, potato and turnip and cook, stirring frequently, for 5 minutes. Add the vegetable stock, salt and pepper and bring to the boil. Lower the heat and add the remaining ingredients. Simmer gently for 8 minutes until the pasta is cooked and the vegetables are just tender. Ladle into bowls and top with lots of freshly ground black pepper.

CHICKPEA, BURGHUL AND PARSLEY SALAD WITH MARINATED LAMB

SERVES 4

3 TABLESPOONS OLIVE OIL
2 TEASPOONS GARAM MASALA
400 G (14 OZ) LAMB BACKSTRAP
SEA SALT
FRESHLY GROUND BLACK PEPPER
200 G (7 OZ) COARSE BURGHUL (BULGUR)
400 G (14 OZ) TIN CHICKPEAS, RINSED
2 GREEN CHILLIES, FINELY CHOPPED
8 SPRING ONIONS (SCALLIONS), THINLY SLICED
LARGE HANDFUL FRESH FLAT-LEAF (ITALIAN) PARSLEY, ROUGHLY CHOPPED
1 GARLIC CLOVE, CRUSHED
3 TABLESPOONS LEMON JUICE
2 TABLESPOONS POMEGRANATE MOLASSES

Mix 1 tablespoon of the olive oil with the garam masala. Brush all over the lamb, season with salt and pepper and set aside for 30 minutes.

Put the burghul in a bowl, cover with hot water and leave to stand for 15 minutes. Drain the burghul, pressing out as much water as possible.

Put the burghul, chickpeas, chilli, spring onions and parsley in a bowl and stir together. Cover with plastic wrap and refrigerate. Stir together the garlic, lemon juice, pomegranate molasses, remaining olive oil, salt and pepper to make a dressing.

Preheat the oven to 180°C (350°F/Gas 4). Heat a large frying pan over medium-high heat and cook the lamb for 2 minutes on each side, or until browned. Transfer to a baking tray and roast the lamb for 6–7 minutes (for medium). Leave for 10 minutes before carving into thin slices. Drizzle the dressing over the salad and serve with the lamb.

"Pomegranate molasses gives this a unique tang. A small teaspoon of brown sugar works well, too."

PAN-FRIED FISH WITH LIME AND CHILLI SLAW

SERVES 4

LIME AND CHILLI SLAW
190 G (6¾ OZ/2½ CUPS) FINELY SHREDDED SAVOY CABBAGE
100 G (3½ OZ) SNOW PEAS (MANGETOUT), FINELY SLICED LENGTHWAYS
1 CELERY STALK, JULIENNED
4 SPRING ONIONS (SCALLIONS), THINLY SLICED
1 TABLESPOON CASTER (SUPERFINE) SUGAR
2 TABLESPOONS OLIVE OIL
2 TABLESPOONS LIME JUICE
2 LONG RED CHILLIES, SEEDED AND CHOPPED

1 TABLESPOON OLIVE OIL
4 X 150 G (5½ OZ) THIN WHITE FISH FILLETS (SUCH AS SNAPPER)
SEA SALT
FRESHLY GROUND BLACK PEPPER

TO SERVE
LIME WEDGES

To make the lime and chilli slaw, put the cabbage, snow peas, celery and spring onion in a bowl and toss together. Cover and refrigerate. Whisk together the sugar, olive oil, lime juice and chillies to make a dressing.

Heat the olive oil in a large frying pan over medium-high heat. Add the fish and cook for 2–3 minutes on each side until golden brown and just cooked through. Toss the coleslaw with the lime and chilli dressing, spoon onto plates and top with pieces of fish. Season well and serve with lime wedges.

"Simple steamed rice, brown or white, works well with this — for those who are eating carbs again. Some of us never gave them up!"

SPICY CHICKEN THIGHS WITH CUCUMBER AND CASHEW SALAD

SERVES 4

3 TABLESPOONS FISH SAUCE
FRESHLY GROUND BLACK PEPPER
3 GARLIC CLOVES, CRUSHED
2 LARGE RED CHILLIES, FINELY MINCED
2 TEASPOONS SUGAR
8 BONELESS SKINLESS CHICKEN THIGHS
2 TABLESPOONS VEGETABLE OIL

CUCUMBER AND CASHEW SALAD
3 TABLESPOONS LIME JUICE
3 TABLESPOONS CASTER (SUPERFINE) SUGAR
200 G (7 OZ) VERMICELLI NOODLES
2 CUCUMBERS, HALVED AND THINLY SLICED
SMALL HANDFUL FRESH MINT LEAVES
4 SPRING ONIONS (SCALLIONS), THINLY SLICED
2 TABLESPOONS CASHEW NUTS, CRUSHED

Whisk the fish sauce, pepper, garlic, chillies and sugar in a bowl. Put the chicken in a separate bowl and pour over half the marinade. Cover with plastic wrap and refrigerate for 20 minutes (keep the rest of the marinade on one side).

Heat the oil in a large frying pan over medium-high heat. Add the chicken, in two batches, and cook for 3 minutes on each side, or until it is cooked through. (Sometimes I put another frying pan on top of the chicken and weigh it down with a couple of tins to make the chicken really crisp.)

While the chicken is cooking, add the lime juice and sugar to the marinade that you set aside. Stir until the sugar has dissolved to make a dressing.

Pour boiling water over the vermicelli and leave for a minute or so until soft. Drain under cold water, place in a large bowl and add the cucumber, mint, spring onions and cashews. Add the dressing, toss well and serve with the sliced chicken.

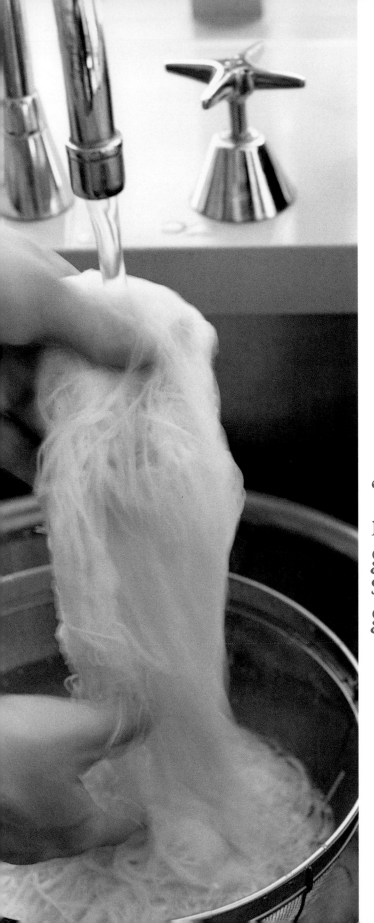

"Give the rice noodles a good rinse to stop them going claggy."

BROCCOLINI AND TOFU SAMBAL

SERVES 4

2 TABLESPOONS PEANUT OIL
375 G (13 OZ) FIRM TOFU, CUT INTO STRIPS
1 ONION, CUT INTO THIN WEDGES
½ TEASPOON SEA SALT
2 GARLIC CLOVES, FINELY CHOPPED
2 BUNCHES BROCCOLINI, CUT INTO LONG FLORETS
2 TEASPOONS SAMBAL OELEK (OPTIONAL)
2 TABLESPOONS LIGHT SOY SAUCE
1 TABLESPOON LEMON JUICE

TO SERVE
STEAMED RICE

Heat half the oil in a wok or frying pan over high heat. Cook the tofu in batches for 2 minutes on each side until it is golden brown. Lift out of the wok and set aside.

Return the wok to high heat and add the remaining oil, onion and salt. Stir-fry for 1 minute, then add the garlic and broccolini and cook for another 2 minutes. Add the sambal oelek and soy sauce and toss through. Add the tofu and stir in the lemon juice. Serve immediately with steamed rice.

"Sambal oelek is an Indonesian chilli paste — great to keep in the fridge. Most supermarkets have it."

MISO, SOBA NOODLE AND SILKEN TOFU BROTH

SERVES 4

2 TABLESPOONS BROWN MISO PASTE
150 G (5½ OZ) SOBA NOODLES
600 G (1 LB 5 OZ/1 BUNCH) BABY BOK CHOY (PAK CHOY)
300 G (10½ OZ) SILKEN FIRM TOFU, CUT INTO SMALL CUBES
FRESH CORIANDER (CILANTRO) LEAVES

Put the miso in a large saucepan with 1.25 litres (44 fl oz/5 cups) of water and whisk together. Bring to the boil, then reduce the heat and simmer gently for 3–4 minutes.

Cook the noodles in a large pan of boiling salted water, following the packet instructions. Add the bok choy to the noodles for the last 30 seconds of cooking. Rinse under cold water and drain well.

Divide the noodles, bok choy and tofu among four serving bowls. Ladle the hot miso into the bowls and top with coriander leaves.

"Tofu's a great protein source and it's not just for hippies these days! Firm tofu is good for stir-fries and barbecues; silken firm is best in soups."

POACHED NECTARINES WITH SWEET VANILLA RICOTTA

SERVES 4

4 NECTARINES
1 LITRE (35 FL OZ/4 CUPS) CRANBERRY JUICE
2 TABLESPOONS CASTER (SUPERFINE) SUGAR
1 CINNAMON STICK
2 WIDE STRIPS LEMON RIND

TO SERVE
SWEET VANILLA RICOTTA, BELOW

Score a small cross in the base of each nectarine. Put the nectarines in a large bowl and pour in enough boiling water to cover them. Leave for 1 minute, then rinse under cold running water. Peel the skin away from the cross and cut each nectarine into quarters, removing the stones.

Put the cranberry juice, sugar, cinnamon and lemon rind in a large saucepan and stir over medium heat until the sugar dissolves. Bring to the boil and simmer for 5 minutes.

Add the nectarines and simmer gently for 5 minutes, or until tender. Remove the nectarines from the poaching liquid with a slotted spoon and set aside to cool. Bring the poaching liquid back to the boil and simmer until reduced by half. Set aside to cool, then pour over the nectarines and chill until ready to serve. Serve the nectarines with a spoonful of the sweet vanilla ricotta.

SWEET VANILLA RICOTTA

MAKES 250 G (9 OZ/1 CUP)

125 G (4½ OZ/½ CUP) FRESH RICOTTA
125 ML (4 FL OZ/½ CUP) CREAMY YOGHURT
1 TABLESPOON CASTER (SUPERFINE) SUGAR
1 TEASPOON VANILLA BEAN PASTE

Mix together the ricotta, yoghurt, sugar and vanilla bean paste.

Mornings are a bit more hectic tuesday since Edie and Inès started school. I'm sure every parent will be smiling as they read this, but I can only imagine what it will be like when we have to get all three ready. I guess we'll cope, just like every other family.

Midweek breakfasts have to be quick and, with five of us round the table, toast — by the time it's buttered and I've found everyone's favourite topping — can be a bit of a bore. So it's great just to add some fresh milk to muesli I've made the day (or even the week) before or fix the girls their favourite porridge.

Inès is the muesli freak of the family and she loves her breakfast at home. Edie's the complete opposite and her idea of heaven would be a croissant in a café. She'll be the next restaurateur in this family. I think she's inherited my foodie genes and some from her maternal grand-mother who was born in France. And Bunny? She's very little and is still in that phase of only eating white food — she'd be happy if every bit of green food was banished from the earth!

Thinking about what to give the girls in their school lunchboxes has made me much more aware of my own health. The idea of a healthy packed lunch works just as well for adults as it does for the kids. I'm not going to get up on my soapbox, but the fat- and sugar-laden processed treats we regularly give our children (not to mention ourselves) these days scare me. It's reassuring to know that in many countries around the world people are now starting to consider the importance of good nutrition for children.

I believe it's really important to develop your children's palates. After all, they are going to be the people you are sharing meals with for the next 20 years, and who wants to dine with fussy eaters? I cook dinner at home every night, so I've got a vested interest in making sure my kids don't request special food and push me into the 'cooking two meals' scenario. Occasionally we'll get them fed early, if we're having friends over for dinner, but Natalie and I are great believers in not giving the girls anything we wouldn't eat ourselves. Special children's menus drive me crazy, too — you don't see kids' menus in Chinatown or at Italian restaurants. Grab an extra plate or two and let them explore the food you eat. If all else fails, any good restaurant should always be able to grill some fresh fish.

When Natalie and I first met we would joke that we were the only people we knew who could spend an hour just working out where to have dinner. Whatever this gene is, I think we've passed it on to our daughters! I remember being in a café with Edie when she ordered a smoked salmon sandwich. There were a couple of those big, briny capers in it which she spat out — not unusual perhaps for a five year-old. But it was only because she preferred the little salted capers she has at home. Pretentious? Moi?

START THE DAY

VANILLA RICE PORRIDGE WITH CARAMELIZED BANANAS

SERVES 4

1 LITRE (35 FL OZ/4 CUPS) MILK
3 TABLESPOONS CASTER (SUPERFINE) SUGAR
1 TEASPOON VANILLA BEAN PASTE
180 G (6½ OZ) ARBORIO RICE
2 BANANAS, THICKLY SLICED ON THE DIAGONAL
1 TABLESPOON SOFT BROWN SUGAR, PLUS EXTRA TO SERVE
1 TABLESPOON BUTTER, CUT INTO SMALL PIECES

Put the milk, sugar and vanilla bean paste in a large saucepan and bring to a simmer over medium heat. Add the rice and stir occasionally to prevent it sticking to the pan. Cook for 30 minutes, or until the rice is tender. Remove from the heat and leave for 5 minutes.

Meanwhile, preheat the grill (broiler) to high. Put the bananas in a shallow ovenproof dish, sprinkle with brown sugar and dot with butter. Grill for 2–3 minutes, or until golden and caramelized.

To serve, spoon the rice pudding into bowls, top with banana and sprinkle with a little brown sugar.

MIX-AND-GO MUESLI

SERVES 8–12

400 G (14 OZ/4 CUPS) ROLLED OATS
220 G (7¾ OZ/2 CUPS) ROLLED BARLEY
75 G (2¾ OZ/1 CUP) BRAN CEREAL
100 G (3½ OZ/⅔ CUP) ALMONDS, CHOPPED
40 G (1½ OZ/⅓ CUP) SUNFLOWER SEEDS
70 G (2½ OZ/½ CUP) PEPITAS (PUMPKIN SEEDS)
80 G (2¾ OZ/⅔ CUP) DRIED PEAR, CHOPPED
80 G (2¾ OZ/⅔ CUP) DRIED STRAWBERRIES

Mix together all the ingredients and store in an airtight container. Serve with milk or fresh berries and yoghurt.

PACKED LUNCHES

SCHOOL LUNCHBOX

MORNING TEA
OATMEAL AND RAISIN COOKIES
250 ML (9 FL OZ) CARTON SKIM MILK

LUNCH
MY FAVOURITE SANDWICH
STEWED APPLE WITH BLUEBERRIES AND YOGHURT

OATMEAL AND RAISIN COOKIES

MAKES 30

150 G (5$\frac{1}{2}$ OZ) UNSALTED BUTTER, SOFTENED
225 G (8 OZ/1 CUP) SOFT BROWN SUGAR
1 EGG, LIGHTLY BEATEN
2 TEASPOONS NATURAL VANILLA EXTRACT
125 G (4$\frac{1}{2}$ OZ/1 CUP) PLAIN (ALL-PURPOSE) FLOUR
1 TEASPOON BAKING POWDER
PINCH OF SALT
235 G (8$\frac{1}{2}$ OZ/2$\frac{1}{3}$ CUPS) ROLLED OATS
125 G (4$\frac{1}{2}$ OZ/1 CUP) RAISINS

Preheat the oven to 180°C (350°F/Gas 4). Line three large baking trays with baking paper.

Cream the butter and sugar together until fluffy and smooth. Add the egg and vanilla extract and beat until smooth. Sift the flour, baking powder and salt into the bowl and mix lightly. Add the oats and raisins and stir together.

Roll tablespoons of the mixture into balls and place on the baking trays. Flatten the balls with a fork dipped in flour. Bake the cookies for 20 minutes, or until pale golden. Remove from the oven and cool on the trays for 5 minutes before transferring to a wire rack to cool completely.

MY FAVOURITE SANDWICH

SERVES 1

2 PIECES WHOLEMEAL OR RYE BREAD
¼ RIPE AVOCADO, LIGHTLY MASHED
SQUEEZE OF LEMON JUICE
2 LETTUCE LEAVES (PERHAPS BUTTER OR ICEBERG)
SHREDDED ROAST OR POACHED CHICKEN FROM THE NIGHT BEFORE

Spread each piece of bread with avocado and squeeze with a little lemon juice to prevent it browning between morning and lunchtime. Top with lettuce leaves and shredded chicken and cut into either two or four, depending on your child's age.

STEWED APPLE WITH BLUEBERRIES AND YOGHURT

SERVES 6

8 GRANNY SMITH APPLES, PEELED, CORED AND CUT INTO EIGHTHS
LOW-FAT YOGHURT
BLUEBERRIES

Put the apples in a saucepan over low heat, with a few tablespoons of water to prevent them catching on the bottom. Cover and cook for 20 minutes, stirring occasionally, until they are softened but not mushy. Leave to cool.

To prepare for the lunchbox, spoon 4 tablespoons into a small container and top with a good tablespoon of yoghurt and a handful of blueberries.

Leftover stewed apple will keep for a week in the fridge and is also great for snacks or on cereal in the morning. It can be blended or mashed for babies.

"Make these
quick pizzas
for dinner, and
make extra
for everyone's
lunch the
next day."

ITALIAN LUNCHBOX

MORNING TEA
WHOLEMEAL GRISSINI WITH CHUNKS OF PARMESAN
SLICED PEAR (SQUEEZE WITH A LITTLE LEMON JUICE TO PREVENT IT TURNING BROWN)

LUNCH
CHEAT'S PIZZA
PEACHES OR NECTARINES WITH STRAWBERRIES

CHEAT'S PIZZA

SERVES 1–2

1 SMALL WHOLEMEAL PITTA BREAD
2 TABLESPOONS TOMATO PASTA SAUCE OR TOMATO PASSATA
FEW STRIPS OF BOTTLED OR HOME-ROASTED RED PEPPERS (CAPSICUMS)
CRUMBLED GOAT'S CHEESE
PROSCIUTTO (OPTIONAL)

Preheat the oven to 240°C (475°F/Gas 8) and put a baking tray in the oven to heat up.

Spread the pitta bread with tomato sauce and top with red pepper and goat's cheese. Put on the tray and bake for 8 minutes until crisp. Leave to cool and then top with prosciutto if you like. Cut into wedges and wrap for the lunchbox.

PICNIC LUNCHBOX

MORNING TEA
FRUIT BREAD SPREAD WITH FRESH RICOTTA, GOAT'S CURD OR ANY SOFT WHITE CHEESE

LUNCH
CRISPY CHICKEN FINGERS
WHITE BEAN, TUNA AND LEMON SALAD
PEACH AND RASPBERRY SLICE

CRISPY CHICKEN FINGERS

SERVES 6

60 G (2¼ OZ/½ CUP) PLAIN (ALL-PURPOSE) FLOUR
SEA SALT
FRESHLY GROUND BLACK PEPPER
3 EGGS
100 G (3½ OZ/1¼ CUPS) FRESH BREADCRUMBS
50 G (1¾ OZ) PARMESAN CHEESE, FINELY GRATED
SMALL HANDFUL FRESH FLAT-LEAF (ITALIAN) PARSLEY, FINELY CHOPPED
4 CHICKEN BREASTS, CUT INTO THIRDS (OR QUARTERS, IF LARGE)
2 TABLESPOONS OLIVE OIL
25 G (1 OZ) BUTTER

Put the flour and a little seasoning in a flat bowl. Beat the eggs in another bowl. Put the breadcrumbs, parmesan, parsley and seasoning in a third bowl and stir together well.

Dip each piece of chicken in the seasoned flour, then the egg and finally in the breadcrumb mixture. Cover and chill for up to 2 hours before cooking.

Heat the olive oil and butter in a large non-stick frying pan over medium-high heat. Add the chicken and cook for about 3 minutes on each side, turning once until lightly golden. You may need to do this in two batches, adding a little more butter and olive oil, if needed.

WHITE BEAN, TUNA AND LEMON SALAD

SERVES 1

85 G (3 OZ/$\frac{1}{2}$ CUP) DRAINED TINNED CANNELLINI BEANS
1 SMALL TIN OF TUNA IN BRINE, DRAINED
$\frac{1}{2}$ CELERY STALK, JULIENNED INTO 5 CM (2 INCH) LENGTHS
1 TABLESPOON SHREDDED FRESH FLAT-LEAF (ITALIAN) PARSLEY
1 SMALL LEMON, PEEL AND PITH REMOVED, THINLY SLICED
2 TEASPOONS EXTRA VIRGIN OLIVE OIL
2 TEASPOONS LEMON JUICE

Layer the beans, tuna, celery, parsley and lemon slices in a small container and drizzle with olive oil and lemon juice.

PEACH AND RASPBERRY SLICE

MAKES 20 PIECES

185 G ($6\frac{1}{2}$ OZ/$1\frac{1}{2}$ CUPS) PLAIN (ALL-PURPOSE) FLOUR
$1\frac{1}{2}$ TEASPOONS BAKING POWDER, PLUS $\frac{1}{2}$ TEASPOON EXTRA
125 G ($4\frac{1}{2}$ OZ) BUTTER, CHILLED AND DICED
115 G (4 OZ/$\frac{1}{2}$ CUP) SOFT BROWN SUGAR
115 G (4 OZ/$\frac{1}{2}$ CUP) CASTER (SUPERFINE) SUGAR
3 RIPE PEACHES, PEELED AND SLICED INTO WEDGES (SEE TIP)
90 G ($3\frac{1}{4}$ OZ/$\frac{3}{4}$ CUP) RASPBERRIES, FRESH OR FROZEN
2 TEASPOONS NATURAL VANILLA EXTRACT
1 EGG, LIGHTLY BEATEN
185 ML (6 FL OZ/$\frac{3}{4}$ CUP) MILK

Preheat the oven to 180°C (350°F/Gas 4). Grease and line the base of a 20 x 30 cm (8 x 12 inch) baking tray. Sift the flour and baking powder into a large bowl and then rub in the butter with your fingertips. Stir in both the sugars. Press half the mixture over the base of the tin. Lay the peaches over the top and sprinkle with raspberries.

Add the vanilla extract, extra baking powder, egg and milk to the rest of the base mixture and stir well — don't worry too much about lumps. Pour evenly over the top of the peaches and raspberries and bake for 1 hour. Cool in the tray, then cut into squares to serve.

TIP: To peel peaches, score a cross in the skin with a sharp knife, then blanch the peaches in boiling water for 30 seconds, refresh in cold water and peel the skin away from the cross.

EASY WEEKDAY DINNERS

SPAGHETTINI WITH FISH, CHILLI AND PARSLEY

SERVES 2

1 TABLESPOON EXTRA VIRGIN OLIVE OIL
2 GARLIC CLOVES, THINLY SLICED
1 LONG RED CHILLI, SEEDED AND FINELY CHOPPED
250 ML (9 FL OZ/1 CUP) DRY WHITE WINE
1 TABLESPOON BUTTER
250 G (9 OZ) FIRM WHITE FISH FILLETS (SUCH AS COD, SNAPPER OR LING), CUT INTO SMALL
    CHUNKS
SEA SALT
200 G (7 OZ) SPAGHETTINI
SMALL HANDFUL FINELY CHOPPED FRESH FLAT-LEAF (ITALIAN) PARSLEY
FRESHLY GROUND BLACK PEPPER

Heat the olive oil in a large pan over medium-low heat. Add the garlic and chilli and cook, stirring, for 1 minute, or until light golden. Add the wine and butter, increase the heat to high and boil for 5 minutes. Add the fish and cook, stirring, for about 2 minutes until just cooked. Season with sea salt and remove from the heat.

Cook the spaghettini in a large pan of lightly salted boiling water until al dente. Drain well.

Add the pasta to the pan with the fish and return to medium heat. Stir gently to coat the spaghettini with sauce. Stir in the parsley and season with black pepper. Serve immediately.

"Nothing beats the smell of garlicky seafood pasta filling the house."

CHILLI BEAN BURRITOS WITH CORN SALSA

SERVES 4

1 TABLESPOON OLIVE OIL
1 ONION, FINELY CHOPPED
1 CELERY STALK, FINELY CHOPPED
2 GARLIC CLOVES, CRUSHED
1 LONG RED CHILLI, FINELY CHOPPED
PINCH OF CAYENNE PEPPER
1 TEASPOON GROUND CORIANDER
1 TEASPOON GROUND CUMIN
2 X 400 G (14 OZ) TINS CHOPPED TOMATOES
2 X 400 G (14 OZ) TINS KIDNEY BEANS, RINSED
JUICE OF 1 LIME
2 TABLESPOONS CHOPPED FRESH CORIANDER (CILANTRO)

TO SERVE
TORTILLAS
CORN SALSA, OPPOSITE
NATURAL YOGHURT

Heat the oil in a large heavy-based pan over medium-low heat. Add the onion and celery and cook, stirring occasionally, for 6–7 minutes until the vegetables are slightly soft. Add the garlic, chilli and spices and cook, stirring, for 1–2 minutes until fragrant.

Add the tomatoes and stir well. Add the kidney beans and bring to the boil, then reduce the heat to very low and simmer, stirring frequently, for 15 minutes, or until thick. Stir in the lime juice and the coriander.

Spoon some bean mixture down the middle of each tortilla and then wrap up firmly. Serve with corn salsa and a spoonful of yoghurt.

CORN SALSA

SERVES 4

1¹/₂ TABLESPOONS OLIVE OIL
300 G (10¹/₂ OZ/1¹/₂ CUPS) CORN KERNELS, CUT FROM THE COB
1 CELERY STALK, DICED
4 SPRING ONIONS (SCALLIONS), FINELY CHOPPED
SMALL HANDFUL FRESH CORIANDER (CILANTRO) LEAVES
1 TABLESPOON LIME JUICE
1 LONG GREEN CHILLI, SEEDED AND FINELY CHOPPED
SEA SALT
FRESHLY GROUND BLACK PEPPER

Heat 1 tablespoon of the oil in a large frying pan over high heat. Add the corn and cook, stirring frequently, for 3–4 minutes. Tip the corn into a large bowl and stir through the celery, spring onion, coriander, lime juice, chilli and remaining oil. Season with sea salt and freshly ground black pepper.

"A small serrated knife is best for cutting corn kernels from the cob. If you can't find fresh, frozen is better than tinned."

"I like to
serve these with
thick yoghurt
instead of sour
cream. I prefer
the texture."

MOROCCAN FISH STEW

SERVES 4

1 TABLESPOON OLIVE OIL
1 LARGE ONION, THINLY SLICED
1 GARLIC CLOVE, CRUSHED
2 TEASPOONS GRATED FRESH GINGER
1 TEASPOON GROUND CUMIN
1 TEASPOON TURMERIC
1 CINNAMON STICK
PINCH OF CAYENNE PEPPER
400 G (14 OZ) TIN CHOPPED TOMATOES
PINCH OF SEA SALT
500 G (1 LB 2 OZ) FIRM WHITE FISH FILLETS (SUCH AS COD, SNAPPER OR LING), CUT
    INTO CHUNKS
400 G (14 OZ) TIN CHICKPEAS, RINSED
2 TEASPOONS HONEY
FRESHLY GROUND BLACK PEPPER

TO SERVE
FRESH CORIANDER (CILANTRO) LEAVES
FLAKED ALMONDS, LIGHTLY TOASTED

Heat the olive oil in a large heavy-based pan over medium-low heat. Add the onion and cook, stirring occasionally, for 5 minutes, or until the onion is translucent. Add the garlic, ginger, cumin, turmeric and cinnamon and cook, stirring, for 2 minutes more, or until fragrant.

Add the cayenne, tomatoes, salt and 250 ml (9 fl oz/1 cup) of water and cook, stirring frequently, for 10 minutes. Add the fish and simmer for 5 minutes, or until the fish is just tender. Add the chickpeas and honey and cook for a further 2–3 minutes. Season to taste. Serve garnished with coriander and flaked almonds.

"While wonderfully light and fragrant, this is rich enough to be satisfying on the coldest night."

STORECUPBOARD PESTO

CORIANDER PESTO

MAKES 250 ML (9 FL OZ/1 CUP)

60 G (2$\frac{1}{4}$ OZ/2 CUPS) FRESH CORIANDER (CILANTRO) LEAVES
80 G (2$\frac{3}{4}$ OZ/$\frac{1}{2}$ CUP) CASHEW NUTS, LIGHTLY TOASTED AND ROUGHLY CHOPPED
2 GARLIC CLOVES, CHOPPED
2 TEASPOONS GRATED FRESH GINGER
1 SMALL RED CHILLI, SEEDED AND CHOPPED
OLIVE OIL
2 TEASPOONS LIME JUICE
SEA SALT
FRESHLY GROUND BLACK PEPPER

Mix the coriander, cashew nuts, garlic, ginger and chilli in a food processor until well blended. With the motor running, add olive oil a little at a time until the pesto has a smooth consistency. Add the lime juice and season with salt and black pepper. Spoon into a sterilized jar and keep in the fridge. Once you've opened the jar, pour a thin layer of oil over the top of the pesto to keep it fresh.

TIP: Sterilize your jars by washing in hot soapy water, or in the dishwasher, and then rinsing well. Place the jars and lids on a baking tray and dry in a warm oven for at least 20 minutes — don't use a tea towel. Leave to cool before using.

WALNUT PESTO

MAKES 250 ML (9 FL OZ/1 CUP)

125 G (4$\frac{1}{2}$ OZ/1 CUP) WALNUTS, LIGHTLY TOASTED AND CHOPPED
2 GARLIC CLOVES, CHOPPED
50 G (1$\frac{3}{4}$ OZ/$\frac{1}{2}$ CUP) GRATED PARMESAN CHEESE
2 TABLESPOONS CHOPPED FRESH FLAT-LEAF (ITALIAN) PARSLEY
OLIVE OIL
SEA SALT
FRESHLY GROUND BLACK PEPPER

Mix the walnuts, garlic, parmesan and parsley in a food processor until well blended. With the motor running, add olive oil a little at a time until the pesto has a smooth consistency. Season with salt and black pepper. Store in a sterilized jar (see Tip, above). Once you've opened the jar, pour a thin layer of oil over the top of the pesto to keep it fresh.

PARSLEY PESTO

MAKES 250 ML (9 FL OZ/1 CUP)

40 G (1½ OZ/2 CUPS) FRESH FLAT-LEAF (ITALIAN) PARSLEY LEAVES
50 G (1¾ OZ/⅓ CUP) PINE NUTS, LIGHTLY TOASTED
50 G (1¾ OZ/½ CUP) GRATED PARMESAN CHEESE
2 GARLIC CLOVES, CHOPPED
2 ANCHOVIES, CHOPPED
1 TEASPOON FINELY GRATED LEMON ZEST
OLIVE OIL
SEA SALT
FRESHLY GROUND BLACK PEPPER

Mix the parsley, pine nuts, parmesan, garlic, anchovies and lemon zest in a food processor until well blended. With the motor running, add olive oil a little at a time until the pesto has a smooth consistency. Season with salt and black pepper. Store in a sterilized jar (see Tip, opposite). Once you've opened the jar, pour a thin layer of oil over the top of the pesto to keep it fresh.

"Try coriander pesto through Asian noodles with chicken, walnut pesto on hot wholemeal pasta with ricotta, and parsley pesto over new potatoes with grilled salmon."

"Once you've opened the jar, pour a thin layer of oil over the pesto to keep it fresh."

STEAK WITH CHERRY TOMATOES AND CANNELLINI BEANS

SERVES 4

3 TABLESPOONS OLIVE OIL
2 X 400 G (14 OZ) TINS CANNELLINI BEANS, RINSED
1 GARLIC CLOVE, SLICED
1/2 TEASPOON CHILLI FLAKES
1 SMALL RED ONION, SLICED INTO THIN WEDGES
250 G (9 OZ) CHERRY TOMATOES
4 X 180 G (6½ OZ) STRIP LOIN (NEW YORK CUT) STEAKS
SEA SALT
FRESHLY GROUND BLACK PEPPER

TO SERVE
1 TABLESPOON BALSAMIC VINEGAR
1 TABLESPOON FRESH OREGANO LEAVES

Preheat the oven to 200°C (400°F/Gas 6). Pour 2 tablespoons of the olive oil, the beans, garlic, chilli flakes, onion and tomatoes into a small baking dish and stir together. Loosely cover with foil and bake for 25 minutes, then remove the foil and bake for a further 5–10 minutes, or until the onion is tender and the tomatoes starting to pucker.

Meanwhile, brush the steaks with the remaining olive oil and season well. Heat a chargrill plate to high and cook the steaks for 3–4 minutes each side (for medium). Leave the steaks to rest for 5 minutes, covered loosely with foil.

When ready to serve, slice each steak into five or six pieces. Serve with the beans and tomatoes, topped with a little balsamic and a sprinkling of oregano.

"Serve this with a rocket and parmesan salad with the lightest drizzle of extra virgin olive oil and a squeeze of lemon."

PORK CUTLETS WITH APPLE SAUCE AND SWEET AND SOUR CABBAGE

SERVES 4

1 TABLESPOON OLIVE OIL
4 PORK LOIN CUTLETS
3 GRANNY SMITH APPLES, PEELED, CORED AND DICED
2 TEASPOONS CASTER (SUPERFINE) SUGAR

TO SERVE
SWEET AND SOUR CABBAGE, BELOW

Preheat the oven to 180°C (350°F/Gas 4). Heat the oil in a large frying pan over high heat. Add the pork cutlets and cook for 2 minutes on each side, or until golden. Transfer the cutlets to a baking tray and bake in the oven for 5 minutes, or until just cooked through.

Meanwhile, return the pan to medium-high heat. Add the apples with 2 tablespoons of water and sprinkle with the sugar. Cook, stirring occasionally, for 6–7 minutes, or until the apples are soft. Serve the pork with the apple sauce and sweet and sour cabbage.

SWEET AND SOUR CABBAGE

SERVES 4

2 TABLESPOONS OLIVE OIL
1 SMALL RED ONION, THINLY SLICED
SEA SALT
1 GARLIC CLOVE, THINLY SLICED
1 TEASPOON GROUND CUMIN
1/2 RED CABBAGE, SHREDDED
1 TABLESPOON SOFT BROWN SUGAR
2 TABLESPOONS BALSAMIC VINEGAR
FRESHLY GROUND BLACK PEPPER

Heat the olive oil in a large pan over medium heat. Add the onion and salt and cook, stirring occasionally, for 5 minutes, or until the onion is soft. Add the garlic and cumin and cook for another minute. Add the cabbage and cook for 15 minutes, tossing often. Add the sugar, vinegar and lots of black pepper and cook for 2 minutes. Serve with pork cutlets and apple sauce.

SALMON WITH MINT AND ROAST POTATO SALAD

SERVES 4

500 G (1 LB 2 OZ) NEW POTATOES, CUT IN HALF (OR QUARTERS, IF LARGE)
2 TABLESPOONS OLIVE OIL, PLUS EXTRA TO BRUSH
SEA SALT
FRESHLY GROUND BLACK PEPPER
125 ML (4 FL OZ/$\frac{1}{2}$ CUP) GREEK YOGHURT
80 ML (2$\frac{1}{2}$ FL OZ/$\frac{1}{3}$ CUP) GOOD-QUALITY MAYONNAISE
2 TABLESPOONS LEMON JUICE
4 X 150 G (5$\frac{1}{2}$ OZ) SALMON FILLETS, WITH SKIN
SMALL HANDFUL FRESH MINT LEAVES
4 SPRING ONIONS (SCALLIONS), SLICED ON THE DIAGONAL

Preheat the oven to 200°C (400°F/Gas 6). Put the potatoes in a large baking tray, drizzle with the olive oil and season well. Roast for 25 minutes, turning once, until golden and crispy.

Meanwhile, stir together the yoghurt, mayonnaise and lemon juice.

Heat a large frying pan over medium-high heat for 2 minutes. Brush the salmon with the extra oil and season well with salt and pepper. Cook the salmon, skin-side-down, for 3 minutes, then turn over and cook for another minute. Remove from the pan and leave to rest for 2 minutes. The salmon should be quite rare and the skin crispy.

Spoon the potatoes onto plates, dollop with the yoghurt dressing and scatter with mint leaves and spring onions. Top with a piece of salmon.

"For a lighter version, use just yoghurt without the mayonnaise."

"Lemon works just as well as lime with this. Chicken legs are an affordable way to use organic chicken."

LIME, PAPRIKA AND HONEY GLAZED CHICKEN

SERVES 4

2 TABLESPOONS PLAIN (ALL-PURPOSE) FLOUR
2 TEASPOONS PAPRIKA
SEA SALT
FRESHLY GROUND BLACK PEPPER
8 CHICKEN LEGS
2 RED ONIONS, CUT INTO WEDGES
2 TABLESPOONS OLIVE OIL
2 TEASPOONS GRATED FRESH GINGER
1 GARLIC CLOVE, CRUSHED
2 TABLESPOONS HONEY
125 ML (4 FL OZ/$\frac{1}{2}$ CUP) CHICKEN STOCK
1 LIME, CUT INTO THIN WEDGES

TO SERVE
STEAMED RICE
ASIAN GREENS
FRESH CORIANDER (CILANTRO) LEAVES

Preheat the oven to 220°C (425°F/Gas 7). Mix the flour and paprika and season with salt and pepper. Dust the chicken legs in the flour and then put in a large roasting tin with the onions. Drizzle with the olive oil and roast for 20 minutes, turning the chicken once during this time.

Mix together the ginger, garlic, honey and chicken stock. Pour over the chicken and add the lime wedges to the tin. Roast for another 10 minutes, or until the chicken is golden and glazed.

Serve with steamed rice, greens and lots of coriander leaves.

ROASTED PLUMS WITH ALMONDS AND CINNAMON ICE CREAM

SERVES 4

2 TEASPOONS GROUND CINNAMON
1 LITRE (35 FL OZ/4 CUPS) VANILLA ICE CREAM, SOFTENED
8 PLUMS, HALVED AND STONES REMOVED
3 TABLESPOONS SOFT BROWN SUGAR
3 TABLESPOONS FLAKED ALMONDS, LIGHTLY TOASTED

Stir the cinnamon into the ice cream and return to the freezer to firm up. Preheat the oven to 200°C (400°F/Gas 6). Put the plums, cut-side-up, in a roasting tin and sprinkle them with brown sugar. Roast for 15 minutes, or until the plums are soft.

Preheat the grill (broiler) to high. Sprinkle the almonds over the plums and place under the grill for 2–3 minutes until the fruit is browned around the edges and the almonds are golden. Leave to cool a little and serve with the cinnamon ice cream.

RAISINS IN LIQUEUR WITH ICE CREAM AND BISCOTTI

SERVES 4–6

125 G (4½ OZ/1 CUP) RAISINS
125 ML (4 FL OZ/½ CUP) MARSALA

TO SERVE
VANILLA ICE CREAM
BISCOTTI

Put the raisins and marsala in a non-metallic bowl, cover and leave in the fridge overnight. Serve with vanilla ice cream and biscotti on the side.

"This is a great way to bring flavour and texture to end-of-season stone fruit."

I'm not sure if I should admit this, but when I was **wednesday** a little boy I'd sometimes sneak a day off school when I wasn't really sick. Mum was pretty cool about it. In fact, I think she liked the company. We'd go to a local café and have those open sandwiches, which were huge in late 70s Melbourne.

Sandwiches you had to eat with a knife and fork seemed like the height of sophistication and were a far cry from the soggy tomato ones I was more familiar with. On a recent business trip to Scandinavia I relived that pleasure with an open prawn sandwich, made with beautiful heavy dark bread, that really was one of the best things I've ever tasted. Sandwiches are the perfect quick lunch. Wherever I am in the world I seek them out, but I have to say it's hard to beat the Brits when it comes to a good sandwich. They invented them, so they ought to know what they're doing.

It's funny how food and travel are so closely linked. I love the exciting and new, and all my travel memories are punctuated by equally clear memories of the food I ate. And I absolutely adore room service! I think it dates back to when I was growing up and my idea of a truly exotic experience was an overnight stay in a country motel, where breakfast came on a tray through a hole in the wall. As a child, the thrill of picking and ticking my own choices on those little room service cards was irresistible.

Looking back, our family holidays were not entirely conventional. My father would book two heavily discounted weeks on a Russian cruise liner, weaving its way around the Fijian islands. And I would spend most of my time in the restaurant. I've got a favourite photo of me with the Russian waitresses in their traditional outfits. I would flirt outrageously with them in an attempt to get more Hawaiian toast — ham, pineapple and cheese!

Another of my not-so-guilty secret pleasures is a really good burger. The great thing about burgers is that they're truly international and, while every country will try to do their own thing (foie gras burger, anyone?), I prefer them simple. I can remember how decadent my first room-service burger tasted in an LA hotel room at the age of 19. Fast-forward to a more recent visit to LA and an amazing pork burger that I enjoyed with my friend Barbara. It was Sunday night, it was winter, and we sat outside. Everything felt perfectly right. That's definitely the most glamorous burger I've ever eaten.

But it's not all room service and glamour! Having a young family brings you right back to earth and the rhythm of our family meals is important to me. Just like everyone else, I often find myself in the supermarket at 5 pm, zoning out in front of all those shelves and thinking "what on earth am I going to make for dinner?" Midweek meals need to be put together quickly — my general rule is that anything that takes longer than 30 minutes isn't an easy dinner. No, make that 20 minutes!

QUICK BREAKFASTS

FRENCH RAISIN TOAST WITH CINNAMON

SERVES 4

4 EGGS
375 ML (13 FL OZ/1½ CUPS) MILK
2 TEASPOONS NATURAL VANILLA EXTRACT
80 G (2¾ OZ/⅓ CUP) CASTER (SUPERFINE) SUGAR
½ TEASPOON GROUND CINNAMON
PINCH OF GROUND NUTMEG
8 SLICES DAY-OLD GOOD-QUALITY RAISIN BREAD
2 TABLESPOONS UNSALTED BUTTER

TO SERVE
MAPLE SYRUP
ICING (CONFECTIONERS') SUGAR, TO DUST

Preheat the oven to 190°C (375°F/Gas 5). Whisk together the eggs, milk, vanilla, sugar, cinnamon and nutmeg and pour into a large flat bowl. Soak each slice of bread in the egg mixture until it is completely saturated.

Heat a large frying pan over medium heat. Add the butter and, once it has started to sizzle, add the bread in batches and cook for 1–2 minutes on each side, or until lightly browned. Lift out the bread onto a baking tray and bake for 10 minutes, or until puffed and golden. Drizzle with maple syrup and dust with icing sugar to serve.

"What is it about French toast that brings out the child in all of us? This is my favourite version."

RASPBERRY AND FIG SMOOTHIE

SERVES 2

125 G (4½ OZ/1 CUP) FRESH RASPBERRIES
2 RIPE FIGS, CHOPPED
125 ML (4 FL OZ/½ CUP) NATURAL YOGHURT
125 ML (4 FL OZ/½ CUP) MILK
2 TEASPOONS HONEY
A HANDFUL OF ICE CUBES

Put all the ingredients in a blender and mix until smooth.

BANANA, STRAWBERRY AND ORANGE SMOOTHIE

SERVES 2

1 LARGE RIPE BANANA
150 G (5½ OZ/1 CUP) STRAWBERRIES, HULLED
250 ML (9 FL OZ/1 CUP) ORANGE JUICE
A HANDFUL OF ICE CUBES

Put all the ingredients in a blender and mix until smooth.

PINEAPPLE, HONEYDEW AND MINT SMOOTHIE

SERVES 2

160 G (5¾ OZ/1 CUP) CHOPPED FRESH PINEAPPLE
160 G (5¾ OZ/1 CUP) CHOPPED HONEYDEW MELON
6 FRESH MINT LEAVES
250 ML (9 FL OZ/1 CUP) PINEAPPLE JUICE
A HANDFUL OF ICE CUBES

Put all the ingredients in a blender and mix until smooth.

NOT-YOUR-EVERYDAY SANDWICHES

HALOUMI OPEN SANDWICH

MAKES 4

1 TABLESPOON OLIVE OIL
8 X 1 CM (½ INCH) THICK SLICES HALOUMI CHEESE
½ LEMON
4 SLICES SOURDOUGH BREAD
4 TABLESPOONS HUMMUS
1 LEBANESE (SHORT) CUCUMBER, CUT INTO LONG WEDGES
ROCKET (ARUGULA) LEAVES
1 RED PEPPER (CAPSICUM), ROASTED, PEELED AND CUT INTO QUARTERS
FRESHLY GROUND BLACK PEPPER

Heat the olive oil in a large frying pan over high heat. Add the haloumi and cook for 2 minutes on each side, or until golden brown. Remove from the pan and squeeze with a little lemon juice.

Toast the sourdough and spread with hummus. Top each slice with some cucumber, rocket leaves, roasted pepper and haloumi. Season generously with black pepper.

"Tzatziki is a lighter, fresh-tasting alternative to the hummus."

L.A. BURGER

SERVES 4

500 G (1 LB 2 OZ) MINCED (GROUND) PORK
½ ONION, GRATED
½ TEASPOON FENNEL SEEDS, LIGHTLY TOASTED AND CRUSHED
40 G (1½ OZ/½ CUP) FRESH WHITE BREADCRUMBS
1 EGG, LIGHTLY BEATEN
1 TABLESPOON CHOPPED FRESH PARSLEY
SEA SALT
FRESHLY GROUND BLACK PEPPER

TO SERVE
HAMBURGER BUNS
ROCKET (ARUGULA) LEAVES
ROASTED RED PEPPER (CAPSICUM)
1 RED ONION, THINLY SLICED
SWEET POTATO FRIES, OPPOSITE

Put the pork, onion, fennel, breadcrumbs, egg and parsley in a large mixing bowl. Season well with sea salt and black pepper and then use your hands to mix everything together thoroughly. Shape the mixture into four patties, then cover and leave in the fridge for 30 minutes.

Heat a frying pan or chargrill pan over high heat. Add the patties and cook for 4–5 minutes on each side until they are browned and cooked through.

Place the patties in hamburger buns and top with rocket leaves, roasted pepper and a few slices of red onion. Serve with sweet potato fries.

SWEET POTATO FRIES

SERVES 4

1 KG (2 LB 4 OZ) SWEET POTATOES, PEELED AND CUT INTO BATONS
2 TABLESPOONS OLIVE OIL
2 TEASPOONS PAPRIKA
1/4 TEASPOON CAYENNE PEPPER
SEA SALT

TO SERVE
LIME WEDGES

Preheat the oven to 230°C (450°F/Gas 8). Toss the sweet potato batons with the olive oil, paprika, cayenne pepper and some sea salt. Scatter them in a single layer on a large baking tray and bake for 30 minutes, stirring occasionally, until the fries are golden brown. Serve with lime wedges.

SALMON TARTINE

SERVES 4

85 G (3 OZ/1/2 CUP) GREEN OLIVES, CUT INTO THIN STRIPS
1 LEMON, PEEL AND PITH REMOVED, CUT INTO SEGMENTS
1 TABLESPOON SALTED BABY CAPERS, RINSED
LARGE HANDFUL FRESH FLAT-LEAF (ITALIAN) PARSLEY LEAVES
8 SLICES SOURDOUGH BREAD
125 G (41/2 OZ/1/2 CUP) FRESH RICOTTA
100 G (31/2 OZ) SMOKED SALMON

Gently toss together the olives, lemon segments, capers and parsley. Toast the sourdough bread until golden. Spread the bread with ricotta and top with smoked salmon. Arrange two slices on each plate and top with some of the olive relish. Serve immediately.

"I'm a sandwich nut. Open, closed or toasted, I can't resist them. With or without fries!"

AFTER-SCHOOL MILK AND COOKIES...
AND SOME GREEN STUFF, TOO

REAL CARAMEL MILKSHAKE

SERVES 2

500 ML (17 FL OZ/2 CUPS) MILK
2 SCOOPS VANILLA ICE CREAM
80 ML (2½ FL OZ/⅓ CUP) CARAMEL SAUCE, BELOW

Put all the ingredients in a blender and mix until smooth.

CARAMEL SAUCE

MAKES 375 ML (13 FL OZ/1½ CUPS)

95 G (3½ OZ/½ CUP) SOFT BROWN SUGAR
250 ML (9 FL OZ/1 CUP) CREAM
1 TEASPOON NATURAL VANILLA EXTRACT
15 G (½ OZ) BUTTER

Put all the ingredients in a small saucepan over medium heat and stir until the sauce comes to a slow boil. Cook, stirring carefully, for 5 minutes over low heat, or until thick and syrupy.

HOT CHOCOLATE

SERVES 4

75 G (2¾ OZ/½ CUP) GOOD-QUALITY CHOCOLATE BUTTONS
1 LITRE (35 FL OZ/4 CUPS) MILK

Pour boiling water into four heatproof glasses and leave for 30 seconds to heat up the glasses. Pour out the water and divide the chocolate buttons among the glasses. Hold each glass on its side and slowly turn it around so the chocolate melts and coats the side of the glass. Warm the milk and pour into the glasses.

GET-SOME-GREENS-IN CRUDITES

SERVES 4–6

250 ML (9 FL OZ/1 CUP) NATURAL YOGHURT
1 TABLESPOON EXTRA VIRGIN OLIVE OIL
1 GARLIC CLOVE, CRUSHED
1 TABLESPOON LEMON JUICE
SEA SALT
FRESHLY GROUND BLACK PEPPER
CUCUMBER BATONS
BLANCHED ASPARAGUS STALKS
YELLOW TEARDROP TOMATOES, HALVED
STRIPS OF YELLOW PEPPER (CAPSICUM)

Mix together the yoghurt, olive oil, garlic, lemon juice, salt and pepper. Serve with cucumber, asparagus, tomatoes and pepper for dipping.

PEANUT BUTTER AND CHOCOLATE CHUNK COOKIES

MAKES 18

150 G (5½ OZ/⅔ CUP) FIRMLY PACKED SOFT BROWN SUGAR
2 TABLESPOONS UNSALTED BUTTER
4 TABLESPOONS CRUNCHY PEANUT BUTTER
1 EGG
1 TEASPOON NATURAL VANILLA EXTRACT
155 G (5½ OZ/1¼ CUPS) PLAIN (ALL-PURPOSE) FLOUR
1 TEASPOON BAKING POWDER
100 G (3½ OZ) GOOD-QUALITY MILK CHOCOLATE, CHOPPED

Preheat the oven to 190°C (375°F/Gas 5). Line two baking trays with baking paper. Beat the sugar, butter and peanut butter with electric beaters until pale and creamy. Add the egg and vanilla and beat until well combined. Sift together the flour and baking powder, fold into the mixture and then stir in the chocolate.

Take heaped tablespoons of dough and roll into balls with your hands. Flatten them slightly and arrange on the trays, leaving some room for spreading. Bake for 10–12 minutes, or until golden brown (the cookies will be soft until they cool). Cool on a wire rack and then store in an airtight container.

ICED JUMBLES

MAKES 30

60 G (2¼ OZ) UNSALTED BUTTER
160 ML (5¼ FL OZ/⅔ CUP) GOLDEN SYRUP
260 G (9¼ OZ/2 CUPS) PLAIN (ALL-PURPOSE) FLOUR
1 TEASPOON BICARBONATE OF SODA (BAKING SODA)
1½ TEASPOONS GROUND GINGER
1 TEASPOON MIXED SPICE
ICING, BELOW

Preheat the oven to 180°C (350°F/Gas 4) and line two baking trays with baking paper. Stir the butter and golden syrup in a pan over medium heat until the butter has melted, then bring to the boil and remove from the heat. Leave to cool for 15 minutes. Sift the flour, bicarbonate of soda and spices together, then stir into the syrup mixture.

Knead the dough on a lightly floured surface until smooth, and then divide into four. Roll each portion into a 3 x 1 cm (1¼ x ½ inch) log and cut into 6 cm (2½ inch) pieces. Place on the trays and bake for 10 minutes, or until light golden. Cool on wire racks and then spread with icing.

ICING

1 EGG WHITE, LIGHTLY BEATEN
240 G (9 OZ/2 CUPS) ICING (CONFECTIONERS') SUGAR
2 TEASPOONS LEMON JUICE
FOOD COLOURING

Stir together the egg white and icing sugar until smooth. Add the lemon juice and a few drops of food colouring and stir well.

"Making the cookies is half the fun, although the kids can get very impatient. Important tip: when baking with children always choose a recipe with a short cooking time!"

EASY WEEKDAY DINNERS

CRISP WHITING WITH TOMATO AND SUMAC SALAD

SERVES 4

125 G (4½ OZ/1 CUP) PLAIN (ALL-PURPOSE) FLOUR, PLUS EXTRA TO DUST
1 TEASPOON BAKING POWDER
½ TEASPOON TURMERIC
SEA SALT
FRESHLY GROUND BLACK PEPPER
ICED WATER
OLIVE OIL, TO SHALLOW-FRY
4 WHITING FILLETS, HALVED LENGTHWAYS
2 LONG RED CHILLIES, FINELY CHOPPED

TO SERVE
LIME WEDGES
TOMATO AND SUMAC SALAD, BELOW

Sift the flour, baking powder and turmeric into a large mixing bowl and season with salt and pepper. Make a well in the centre and then whisk in enough iced water to make a smooth batter.

Pour 5 cm (2 inches) of oil into a saucepan and place over high heat. Dust the fish in the extra flour and then dip into the batter, allowing the excess to drip off.

Carefully lower the fish into the hot oil in small batches and fry until golden brown. Remove with a slotted spoon and drain on paper towels. Scatter with chilli and serve with lime wedges and the salad.

TOMATO AND SUMAC SALAD

SERVES 4

250 G (9 OZ) CHERRY TOMATOES, HALVED
4 LARGE-BULB SPRING ONIONS (SALAD ONIONS), THINLY SLICED
SMALL HANDFUL FRESH MINT LEAVES
SEA SALT
FRESHLY GROUND BLACK PEPPER
2 TABLESPOONS EXTRA VIRGIN OLIVE OIL
SUMAC, TO SPRINKLE

Toss together the tomatoes, onions and mint, season with salt and pepper and pile onto a serving platter. Drizzle with the olive oil and sprinkle with sumac.

SPAGHETTI WITH GARLIC AND SPINACH

SERVES 4

400 G (14 OZ) SPAGHETTI
80 ML (2½ FL OZ/⅓ CUP) EXTRA VIRGIN OLIVE OIL
6 GARLIC CLOVES, THINLY SLICED
SLICED RED CHILLI, TO TASTE (I LIKE TO USE 2 SMALL ONES)
80 ML (2½ FL OZ/⅓ CUP) WHITE WINE
90 G (3¼ OZ/2 CUPS) BABY ENGLISH SPINACH
SEA SALT
SMALL HANDFUL FINELY CHOPPED FRESH FLAT-LEAF (ITALIAN) PARSLEY

TO SERVE
GRATED PARMESAN CHEESE

Cook the spaghetti in a large pan of boiling salted water until al dente. Meanwhile, put the olive oil, garlic and chilli in a frying pan over medium heat and cook, stirring often, for about 5 minutes until the garlic is golden. Add the wine and cook, stirring, for 20 seconds. Add the drained pasta and spinach and toss to coat it well. Season with sea salt and sprinkle with parsley, then serve with lots of grated parmesan.

"I invariably use a spelt or wholewheat pasta (I really enjoy the nuttiness and texture, aside from the health benefits) and throw in a handful of something green, like broccoli, asparagus or spinach."

STIR-FRIED CHICKEN WITH PEANUTS AND CUCUMBER

SERVES 4

2 TABLESPOONS PEANUT OIL
500 G (1 LB 2 OZ) CHICKEN BREASTS, DICED
2 TABLESPOONS CHINESE RICE WINE
2 TABLESPOONS SOY SAUCE
2 TEASPOONS SESAME OIL
2 TEASPOONS CASTER (SUPERFINE) SUGAR
1 TEASPOON CORNFLOUR (CORNSTARCH)
1 ONION, DICED
2 TEASPOONS FINELY GRATED FRESH GINGER
1 SMALL RED AND 1 SMALL GREEN PEPPER (CAPSICUM), DICED
2 LEBANESE (SHORT) CUCUMBERS, HALVED, SEEDED AND DICED

TO SERVE
STEAMED RICE
UNSALTED ROASTED PEANUTS, CHOPPED

Heat 1 tablespoon of the oil in a large wok or frying pan over high heat. Cook the chicken in batches for 3–4 minutes, or until golden, then remove from the wok.

Mix together the rice wine, soy sauce, sesame oil, sugar and cornflour. Return the wok to medium-high heat. Add the rest of the oil, the onion and ginger and stir-fry for 1–2 minutes, then add the pepper and cucumber and stir-fry for another 2 minutes. Return the chicken to the wok, add the sauce and stir-fry for another couple of minutes.

Serve immediately with steamed rice and chopped peanuts.

"This makes a great TV dinner with steamed rice."

TUNA DAUBE

SERVES 4

4 TUNA STEAKS (ABOUT 180 G/6½ OZ EACH)
SEA SALT
FRESHLY GROUND BLACK PEPPER
3 TABLESPOONS EXTRA VIRGIN OLIVE OIL
2 ONIONS, THINLY SLICED
1 TABLESPOON FINELY CHOPPED PARSLEY, PLUS 1 TABLESPOON EXTRA
4 ANCHOVIES, ROUGHLY CHOPPED
1 SMALL RED CHILLI, THINLY SLICED
4 GARLIC CLOVES, SLICED
400 G (14 OZ) TIN CHOPPED TOMATOES
375 ML (13 FL OZ/1½ CUPS) CHICKEN STOCK OR WATER
2 BAY LEAVES, FRESH OR DRIED

TO SERVE
SHREDDED FRESH BASIL LEAVES

Season the tuna well. Heat 1 tablespoon of the oil in a large flameproof casserole dish over high heat, add the tuna and cook for 2 minutes on one side and 1 minute on the other. Remove and set aside.

Reduce the heat to medium, add the rest of the oil and the onions and cook for 10 minutes, stirring occasionally, until softened. Add the parsley, anchovies, chilli and garlic and cook for another minute. Add the tomatoes, chicken stock and bay leaves and simmer, covered, for 25 minutes. Return the tuna to the dish, put the lid back on and remove from the heat. Leave for 5 minutes, then sprinkle with shredded basil leaves to serve.

"A traditional daube is made with beef and cooks for hours — this is a quick midweek version."

SAUSAGES WITH CARAMELIZED ONIONS AND PARMESAN MASH

SERVES 4

4 RED ONIONS, QUARTERED (OR CUT INTO EIGHTHS, IF LARGE)
2 TABLESPOONS SOFT BROWN SUGAR
$1/_2$ TEASPOON RED CHILLI FLAKES
SEA SALT
FRESHLY GROUND BLACK PEPPER
2 TABLESPOONS EXTRA VIRGIN OLIVE OIL
2 TABLESPOONS RED WINE VINEGAR OR BALSAMIC VINEGAR
8 GOOD-QUALITY SAUSAGES

TO SERVE
PARMESAN MASH, BELOW

Preheat the oven to 200°C (400°F/Gas 6). Put the onions in a baking dish and sprinkle with the sugar, chilli flakes, salt and pepper. Drizzle with olive oil and vinegar and bake for 35 minutes.

Cook the sausages in a frying pan over medium-high heat for about 15 minutes until well browned. Serve with the caramelized onions and parmesan mash.

PARMESAN MASH

SERVES 4

800 G (1 LB 12 OZ) DESIREE POTATOES, PEELED AND CUT INTO CHUNKS
SEA SALT
125 ML ($4^1/_2$ FL OZ/$1/_2$ CUP) MILK
25 G (1 OZ) BUTTER
35 G ($1^1/_4$ OZ/$1/_3$ CUP) FINELY GRATED PARMESAN CHEESE
FRESHLY GROUND BLACK PEPPER

Cook the potatoes in boiling salted water until tender, then drain and mash. Heat the milk and butter in a saucepan until the butter has melted and then beat into the mash until smooth. Add the parmesan and beat well. Season with salt and pepper.

CRISP-SKIN SALMON WITH SWEET CHILLI DRESSING

SERVES 4

200 G (7 OZ) SNOW PEAS (MANGETOUT), BLANCHED
SMALL HANDFUL CORIANDER (CILANTRO) LEAVES
4 SPRING ONIONS (SCALLIONS), SLICED ON THE DIAGONAL
2 TABLESPOONS SOFT BROWN SUGAR
2 TABLESPOONS CASTER (SUPERFINE) SUGAR
2 TABLESPOONS FISH SAUCE
2 TABLESPOONS LIME JUICE
1 RED CHILLI, FINELY CHOPPED
4 X 180 G (6½ OZ) SALMON FILLETS, WITH SKIN
1 TABLESPOON LIGHT-FLAVOURED OIL (SUCH AS CANOLA)

Toss together the snow peas, coriander and spring onions.

Stir the sugars and 2 tablespoons of water in a small saucepan over low heat until the sugars have dissolved. Cook over medium heat until lightly golden. Remove from the heat and stir in the fish sauce, lime juice and chilli.

Brush the salmon with the oil. Heat a large frying pan over medium-high heat for 2 minutes and then cook the fish, skin-side-down, for 2 minutes until it is crispy. Turn the fish over and cook for 1 minute. Spoon the salad onto plates with the fish and pour the dressing over the top.

"Make sure your pan is very hot before you put the salmon in. That way the skin will become deliciously crisp."

"Stir-fry secrets:
- get everything
    sliced;
- get noodles
    soaked;
- have sauces
    mixed;
then dinner
only takes
5 minutes."

BEEF AND NOODLE STIR-FRY WITH ASIAN GREENS

SERVES 4

375 G (13 OZ) FRESH RICE NOODLES
2 TEASPOONS SESAME OIL
3 TABLESPOONS OYSTER SAUCE
2 TABLESPOONS DARK SOY SAUCE
1½ TABLESPOONS DRY SHERRY OR CHINESE RICE WINE
3 TABLESPOONS CHICKEN STOCK
2 TEASPOONS SUGAR
1 TABLESPOON PEANUT OIL
600 G (1 LB 5 OZ) BEEF FILLET OR RUMP, THINLY SLICED
4 CM (1½ INCH) PIECE OF FRESH GINGER, JULIENNED OR GRATED
1 BUNCH CHINESE BROCCOLI (GAI LARN), STALKS REMOVED AND HALVED, LEAVES HALVED

Cover the noodles in boiling salted water according to the packet instructions. Drain and toss with the sesame oil. Meanwhile, stir together the oyster sauce, soy sauce, sherry, stock and sugar.

Heat a wok or large frying pan over high heat. Add the peanut oil and, when smoking, add the beef in two batches, cooking for 1 minute to seal and brown. Remove and set aside. Add the ginger and Chinese broccoli, adding a little extra oil if needed, and stir-fry for 2 minutes. Add the beef and sauce and cook for another minute to slightly reduce the sauce.

Either toss the noodles through the sauce in the wok, or spoon them into bowls and top with the beef stir-fry.

SPICY CHICKEN MEATBALLS

SERVES 4

3 TABLESPOONS OLIVE OIL
1 SMALL ONION, FINELY DICED
2 GARLIC CLOVES, CRUSHED
½ TEASPOON GROUND CORIANDER
1 RED CHILLI, THINLY SLICED
500 G (1 LB 2 OZ) MINCED (GROUND) CHICKEN
3 TABLESPOONS FRESH BREADCRUMBS
50 G (1¾ OZ) PANCETTA, CHOPPED
2 TABLESPOONS CHOPPED FRESH FLAT-LEAF (ITALIAN) PARSLEY
SEA SALT
500 G (1 LB 2 OZ) CHERRY TOMATOES, HALVED
FRESHLY GROUND BLACK PEPPER
125 ML (4 FL OZ/½ CUP) CHICKEN STOCK

TO SERVE
500 G (1 LB 2 OZ) WHOLEWHEAT FUSILLI, COOKED
PARMESAN SHAVINGS

Preheat the oven to 200°C (400°F/Gas 6). Heat 1 tablespoon of the oil in a saucepan over medium-high heat. Add the onion and garlic and cook, stirring, for 5 minutes, or until the onion is soft. Add the coriander and chilli and cook for 1 minute.

Put the chicken in a bowl with the breadcrumbs, pancetta, parsley and salt. Add the spiced onion and mix well with your hands. Refrigerate for 30 minutes to firm the mixture. Wet your hands with cold water to stop the mixture sticking and roll it into small meatballs.

Put the cherry tomatoes on a baking tray lined with baking paper, drizzle with 1 tablespoon olive oil and season with salt and pepper. Put the meatballs on a second lined tray and drizzle with the remaining oil. Roast the tomatoes and meatballs in the oven for 15–20 minutes, or until the meatballs are golden and the tomatoes starting to pucker.

Put the stock and tomatoes in a saucepan and add the meatballs. Simmer for 5 minutes and season to taste before spooning over pasta and serving with parmesan shavings.

GOLDEN SYRUP PUDDINGS

SERVES 4

125 G (4½ OZ/1 CUP) SELF-RAISING FLOUR
1 TEASPOON GROUND GINGER
95 G (3½ OZ/½ CUP) SOFT BROWN SUGAR
60 G (2¼ OZ) UNSALTED BUTTER, MELTED
1 EGG, LIGHTLY BEATEN
125 ML (4 FL OZ/½ CUP) MILK
1 TABLESPOON GOLDEN SYRUP
1 TEASPOON NATURAL VANILLA EXTRACT

SAUCE
95 G (3½ OZ/½ CUP) SOFT BROWN SUGAR
2 TABLESPOONS GOLDEN SYRUP
310 ML (10¾ FL OZ/1¼ CUPS) BOILING WATER

Preheat the oven to 190°C (375°F/Gas 5). Lightly butter four 250 ml (9 fl oz/1 cup) ovenproof dishes. Mix the flour, ginger and sugar in a large bowl. Add the melted butter, egg, milk, golden syrup and vanilla and stir until everything is well combined. Spoon into the dishes.

Mix together all the sauce ingredients and carefully, using the back of a spoon, pour the sauce evenly over the batter in the dishes. Bake for 20 minutes, or until the sponge is firm and golden.

BAKED NECTARINE CRUMBLES

SERVES 4

4 FIRM RIPE NECTARINES, HALVED AND STONES REMOVED
2 TABLESPOONS PLAIN (ALL-PURPOSE) FLOUR
2 TABLESPOONS BUTTER, DICED
35 G (1¼ OZ/⅓ CUP) ROLLED OATS
1 TABLESPOON SOFT BROWN SUGAR
1 TEASPOON GROUND CINNAMON
1 TABLESPOON BUTTER, DICED, EXTRA

TO SERVE
CREAM OR ICE CREAM

Preheat the oven to 180°C (350°F/Gas 4). Put the nectarines, cut-side-up, in a large shallow baking tray. Sift the flour into a bowl and rub in the butter with your fingertips until the mixture is crumbly. Add the oats, sugar and cinnamon and stir well. Spoon the crumble over the nectarines, dot with the extra butter and bake for 15–20 minutes, or until the nectarines are soft and the crumble is golden brown. Serve with cream or ice cream.

Entertaining. It sounds very formal somehow, doesn't it? It used to be thursday about setting the table the night before, putting candles in the candelabra and polishing the silver. When I think back to my parents' 70s dinner parties, I think of lace tablecloths, red paper napkins and red roses.

I guess times have changed. Would our parents have entertained on a Thursday evening? Those elaborately-styled dinner parties were very much a Saturday night thing, taking a whole day of preparation (and, sometimes, a whole week of anticipation). I suppose barbies were more relaxed, but they were strictly 'weekends only' as well. Friends didn't tend to drop in after work for a bite to eat and a glass of wine like they do today.

I've always liked Thursday night because you can kid yourself it's the weekend (at least until Friday morning you can!) and it's great to have a few friends over for a kitchen dinner. It might just be a pizza with some fresh basil and olives thrown on top. Or simple pasta with great bread and a dessert I've bought from the deli on my way home. I love the whole idea of mixing some good take-away foods with a few dishes I make at home. Why make it a chore, when it should be a pleasure? Sometimes it's good to treat friends to something really special, but the Thursday night rule is definitely 'make it easy'. Minimum preparation, maximum conversation.

With casual entertaining I like to put together a meal where a few of us can be in the kitchen at once and people can actually help with the preparation. I know when I go for dinner I always seem to end up in the kitchen doing things (as far as I'm concerned, it's the best place to be at any party). Friends enjoy helping, they enjoy chatting to you while everything comes together... in fact, I've come to the conclusion that most of us just feel more relaxed in the kitchen than sitting around the candelabra!

If it's winter, I might find the time and energy to prepare a curry. Everyone loves a curry and they say it's an off-duty chef's favourite food. It must be all that complex layering of flavours. I first went to India in 1989, when I was 19 years old and, to be honest, at that time finding a good curry in Goa was probably the last thing on my mind. But a love of Indian food has stayed with me. I prefer the hot, vinegary sourness of southern Indian dishes to the sweeter, richer, creamier curries of the north and, much as I love traditional accompaniments like rice, bread and pappadums, I'll choose cool yoghurt and a simple salad. To me, salad is the perfect partner for a curry — it balances that smooth, slow-cooked richness with something fresh and alive.

BREAKFAST ON THE RUN

REAL MUESLI BARS

MAKES 16

350 G (12 OZ/3½ CUPS) ROLLED OATS
30 G (1 OZ/½ CUP) SHREDDED COCONUT
50 G (1¾ OZ/½ CUP) FLAKED ALMONDS
45 G (1¾ OZ/½ CUP) WHEATGERM
30 G (1 OZ/¼ CUP) SESAME SEEDS
35 G (1¼ OZ/¼ CUP) SUNFLOWER SEEDS
55 G (2 OZ/⅓ CUP) CHOPPED DRIED APRICOTS
185 ML (6 FL OZ/¾ CUP) HONEY
55 G (2 OZ/¼ CUP) FIRMLY PACKED SOFT BROWN SUGAR
125 ML (4 FL OZ/½ CUP) VEGETABLE OIL

Preheat the oven to 130°C (250°F/Gas 1) and lightly grease and line a 35 x 25 cm (14 x 10 inch) tin. Put the oats, coconut, almonds, wheatgerm, seasame seeds, sunflower seeds and apricots in a bowl.

Put the honey, sugar and oil in a small pan and stir over medium heat until the sugar has dissolved. Pour this over the dry ingedients in the bowl and stir until everything is well combined, mixing with your hands if necessary.

Press the mixture into the tin and bake for 50 minutes, or until golden brown. Cut into bars while still warm.

BERRY YOGHURT MUFFINS

MAKES 12

185 G (6½ OZ/1½ CUPS) SELF-RAISING FLOUR
150 G (5½ OZ/1 CUP) WHOLEMEAL SELF-RAISING FLOUR
1 TEASPOON GROUND CINNAMON
155 G (5½ OZ/¾ CUP) FIRMLY PACKED SOFT BROWN SUGAR
250 ML (9 FL OZ/1 CUP) BUTTERMILK
125 ML (4 FL OZ/½ CUP) LOW-FAT NATURAL YOGHURT
2 EGGS, LIGHTLY BEATEN
2 TABLESPOONS VEGETABLE OIL
440 G (15 OZ/2 CUPS) CHOPPED MIXED BERRIES (I LIKE STRAWBERRIES AND RASPBERRIES)

Preheat the oven to 180°C (350°F/Gas 4). Line a 12-hole 125 ml (4 fl oz/½ cup) capacity muffin tin with paper cases.

Sift the two flours and cinnamon together into a large bowl. Stir in the sugar and then make a well in the centre. Pour the buttermilk, yoghurt, eggs and oil into a large bowl and whisk with a fork until just combined. Pour into the well in the dry ingredients and stir with a wooden spoon until just combined. Add the berries and stir until just combined (do not overmix or your muffins will be tough). Spoon into the muffin tin and bake for 20 minutes, or until golden.

"These freeze brilliantly and are perfect for the kids' lunchboxes — or even mine!"

KIDS' MEALS

EGG NOODLES WITH TOFU AND GREEN BEANS

SERVES 4

375 G (13 OZ) FRESH EGG NOODLES
2 TABLESPOONS SOY SAUCE
1 TABLESPOON LIME JUICE
1 TABLESPOON FISH SAUCE
2 TEASPOONS SOFT BROWN SUGAR
1 TABLESPOON LIGHT-FLAVOURED OIL (SUCH AS CANOLA)
4 CM (1½ INCH) PIECE OF FRESH GINGER, PEELED, JULIENNED OR GRATED
200 G (7 OZ) GREEN BEANS, SLICED ON THE DIAGONAL
300 G (10½ OZ) TOFU, CUT INTO SMALL BATONS

TO SERVE
CUCUMBER BATONS
CHOPPED CASHEW NUTS

Cook the egg noodles in boiling water according to the packet instructions, drain and set aside. Meanwhile, stir together the soy sauce, lime juice, fish sauce and sugar.

Heat a wok or large frying pan over high heat. Add the oil and, when smoking, add the ginger and green beans and stir-fry for 2 minutes. Add the tofu and stir-fry until golden. Add the sauce and cook for 1 minute until slightly reduced. Add the noodles to the wok and toss well, or put the noodles in bowls and top with the sauce. Serve with cucumber and cashews sprinkled on top.

STIR-FRIED PORK WITH HOISIN AND GREENS

SERVES 4

2 TEASPOONS CORNFLOUR (CORNSTARCH)
1 TABLESPOON SESAME OIL
1 TEASPOON CHINESE FIVE-SPICE
400 G (14 OZ) PORK LEG STEAK, CUT INTO THIN STRIPS
2 TABLESPOONS SOY SAUCE
2 TABLESPOONS HOISIN SAUCE
3 TABLESPOONS CHICKEN STOCK
1 TABLESPOON PEANUT OIL
3 CM (1 INCH) PIECE OF FRESH GINGER, PEELED AND CUT INTO THIN STRIPS
1 BUNCH BROCCOLINI, CUT INTO LONG FLORETS
6 SPRING ONIONS (SCALLIONS), CHOPPED

TO SERVE
STEAMED JASMINE RICE

Mix together the cornflour, sesame oil and five-spice. Put the pork in a non-metallic bowl, pour the cornflour mixture over the top and stir to coat. Cover and refrigerate for 20 minutes.

Mix together the soy, hoisin and chicken stock. Heat the peanut oil in a large wok or frying pan over high heat. Add the ginger, broccolini and spring onions to the wok and stir-fry for 2 minutes, or until the broccolini is just cooked. Remove from the wok.

Add the pork to the wok and stir-fry for 2–3 minutes, or until the pork is light golden. Return the vegetables to the wok, add the sauce and stir-fry for 2 minutes. Serve with jasmine rice.

"The sweetness of hoisin is perfect for young palates and a great intro to grown-up flavours."

BAKED TOMATO AND MOZZARELLA PASTA

SERVES 4

1 TABLESPOON OLIVE OIL
1 SMALL ONION, FINELY CHOPPED
1 GARLIC CLOVE, CRUSHED
1 SMALL CARROT, DICED
1 CELERY STALK, DICED
400 G (14 OZ) TIN CHOPPED TOMATOES
45 G (1¾ OZ/¼ CUP) SMALL BLACK OLIVES, PITTED
SEA SALT
FRESHLY GROUND BLACK PEPPER
300 G (10½ OZ) COOKED SHORT PASTA (SUCH AS FUSILLI OR PENNE)
75 G (2¾ OZ) FRESH MOZZARELLA CHEESE, TORN INTO PIECES

Preheat the oven to 180°C (350°F/Gas 4). Heat the olive oil in a pan over medium-low heat and cook the onion, stirring, for 5 minutes, or until soft. Add the garlic, carrot and celery and cook, stirring, for 5 minutes more.

Add the tomatoes and bring to the boil, then reduce the heat to low and simmer for 5 minutes. Stir in the olives, season with salt and pepper and remove from the heat.

Stir the tomato sauce through the cooked pasta and spoon into a casserole dish. Dot with mozzarella and bake for 30 minutes until the cheese is melted and bubbling.

"I've never been a great fan of macaroni cheese — this is my equivalent. It's economical, too, if you use leftover pasta."

OVEN-BAKED CHICKEN AND ASPARAGUS RISOTTO

SERVES 4

2 TABLESPOONS OLIVE OIL
500 G (1 LB 2 OZ) BONELESS CHICKEN BREASTS, CUT INTO THIN STRIPS
1 ONION, FINELY CHOPPED
1 GARLIC CLOVE, CRUSHED
1 TEASPOON FINELY GRATED LEMON ZEST
250 G (9 OZ) ARBORIO RICE
750 ML (26 FL OZ/3 CUPS) CHICKEN STOCK
175 G (6 OZ/1 BUNCH) ASPARAGUS, SLICED ON THE DIAGONAL
35 G (1¼ OZ/⅓ CUP) GRATED PARMESAN CHEESE, PLUS EXTRA TO SERVE
SEA SALT
FRESHLY GROUND BLACK PEPPER

Preheat the oven to 180°C (350°F/Gas 4). Heat 1 tablespoon of the olive oil in a large flameproof casserole over high heat. Add the chicken and cook, stirring frequently, for 3–4 minutes, or until golden brown. Remove from the casserole and set aside.

Add the remaining olive oil and the onion to the casserole and cook, stirring occasionally, for 5 minutes, or until the onion is soft. Add the garlic and lemon zest and cook, stirring, for 30 seconds. Add the rice and stir to coat in the oil. Add the stock and bring to the boil, stirring occasionally.

Cover the casserole and put in the oven for 15 minutes. Add the asparagus, return the chicken to the casserole and bake for a further 3–4 minutes, or until the asparagus is bright green and just tender. Stir in the parmesan and season with salt and pepper, before serving with extra parmesan.

"The best thing about this dish is that it gives you time to bath the kids while it's in the oven... or have a glass of wine!"

CREAMY MUSHROOM AND PROSCIUTTO PASTA

SERVES 4

400 G (14 OZ) TAGLIATELLI OR PAPPARDELLE
1 TABLESPOON OLIVE OIL
1 GARLIC CLOVE, CRUSHED
4 SLICES PROSCIUTTO, CHOPPED
200 G (7 OZ) BUTTON MUSHROOMS, SLICED
80 ML (2½ FL OZ/⅓ CUP) CHICKEN STOCK
80 ML (2½ FL OZ/⅓ CUP) CREAM
SEA SALT
FRESHLY GROUND BLACK PEPPER
1 TABLESPOON CHOPPED FRESH PARSLEY

TO SERVE
GRATED PARMESAN CHEESE

Cook the pasta in a large pan of lightly salted boiling water until al dente.

Meanwhile, heat the olive oil in a frying pan over medium-high heat. Add the garlic and prosciutto and cook, stirring occasionally, for 3–4 minutes, or until the prosciutto is crisp. Add the mushrooms and cook for 4 minutes, or until they are light golden. Add the stock and let it reduce by half, then add the cream and simmer for a further 2 minutes, stirring occasionally.

Drain the pasta, add to the sauce and toss to coat. Season with salt and pepper and stir in the parsley. Serve immediately with grated parmesan.

FRIENDS FOR DINNER

WINTER DINNER

CHICKEN, TOMATO AND FENNEL CASSEROLE

SERVES 4

2 TABLESPOONS OLIVE OIL
8 CHICKEN THIGH CUTLETS ON THE BONE, WITH SKIN
1 ONION, SLICED
1 LARGE FENNEL BULB, TRIMMED AND THINLY SLICED
2 GARLIC CLOVES, CRUSHED
1/2 TEASPOON CRUSHED FENNEL SEEDS
2 TEASPOONS PAPRIKA
1/2 TEASPOON SAFFRON THREADS, SOAKED IN 1 TABLESPOON WATER
WIDE STRIP OF ORANGE RIND
400 G (14 OZ) TIN CHOPPED TOMATOES
500 ML (17 FL OZ/2 CUPS) CHICKEN STOCK
1 RED PEPPER (CAPSICUM), ROASTED AND THINLY SLICED
2 TEASPOONS HONEY
SEA SALT
FRESHLY GROUND BLACK PEPPER

Heat the oil in a large heavy-based pan over medium-high heat. Add the chicken (in batches, if necessary) and brown for 2–3 minutes on each side. Remove from the pan and set aside. Drain most of the oil from the pan, leaving just about 1 tablespoon.

Reduce the heat to medium and add the onion and fennel to the pan. Cook, stirring occasionally, for 7–8 minutes, or until the vegetables are soft. Add the garlic, fennel seeds and paprika and cook, stirring, for another minute. Add the saffron with its liquid, the orange rind, tomatoes, stock and pepper to the pan and stir well. Return the chicken pieces to the pan, bring to the boil and then reduce the heat to low. Cover and simmer for 30 minutes, or until the chicken is cooked through and tender. Skim any oil from the top of the casserole. Stir in the honey and season with salt and pepper.

GARLIC TOASTS

SERVES 4

6 GARLIC CLOVES, PEELED
2 TABLESPOONS OLIVE OIL
SEA SALT
FRESHLY GROUND BLACK PEPPER
2 TABLESPOONS BUTTER
1 TABLESPOON CHOPPED FRESH FLAT-LEAF (ITALIAN) PARSLEY
8 SLICES CROSTINI OR BAGUETTE

Preheat the oven to 180°C (350°F/Gas 4). Put the garlic and olive oil in a small roasting tin and season with salt and pepper. Cover with foil and roast for 20 minutes. Remove from the oven and leave to cool slightly, then put the garlic in a bowl and mash with a fork. Add the butter and parsley and mash together. Put the bread on a baking tray, spread with the garlic butter and bake for 5–10 minutes, or until crisp. Serve with the chicken, tomato and fennel casserole.

WATERCRESS, APPLE AND WITLOF SALAD

SERVES 4

LEAVES FROM 1 BUNCH WATERCRESS
2 WITLOF (CHICORY, BELGIAN ENDIVE), OUTER LEAVES DISCARDED
1 APPLE
JUICE OF 1/2 LEMON
2 TEASPOONS CHAMPAGNE VINEGAR
2 TEASPOONS DIJON MUSTARD
1 1/2 TABLESPOONS OLIVE OIL
SEA SALT
FRESHLY GROUND BLACK PEPPER

Put the watercress and witlof leaves in a salad bowl. Cut the apple into quarters, remove the core and slice the apple thinly. Sprinkle with a little of the lemon juice and add to the salad leaves.

Whisk together the remaining lemon juice, vinegar, mustard and olive oil. Season with salt and pepper and drizzle over the salad.

"Baking the garlic might be extra work but it mellows the flavour and makes a world of difference."

AFTER-WORK DINNER PARTY

VEAL CUTLETS WITH SHALLOTS, MUSHROOMS AND BALSAMIC

SERVES 4

2 TABLESPOONS OLIVE OIL
8 VEAL CUTLETS, FRENCH TRIMMED
8 SMALL FRENCH SHALLOTS, PEELED
100 G (3½ OZ) PANCETTA, RIND REMOVED, CUT INTO LARDONS
200 G (7 OZ) SWISS BROWN MUSHROOMS, TRIMMED
80 ML (2½ FL OZ/⅓ CUP) WHITE WINE
150 ML (5 FL OZ) CHICKEN STOCK
1 TABLESPOON BALSAMIC VINEGAR
1 TABLESPOON COLD BUTTER, DICED
SEA SALT
FRESHLY GROUND BLACK PEPPER

TO SERVE
90 G (3¼ OZ/2 CUPS) BABY ENGLISH SPINACH
PARMESAN MASH, PAGE 105

Heat 1 tablespoon of the olive oil in a large frying pan over high heat. Add the cutlets and cook for 2–3 minutes on each side, or until golden brown. Remove, cover and set aside.

Return the pan to medium-high heat and add the remaining olive oil and the shallots. Cook, stirring occasionally, for 4–5 minutes until the shallots are golden. Add the pancetta and whole mushrooms and cook, stirring frequently, for a further 6–7 minutes, or until the pancetta is crisp. Add the wine and let it bubble until reduced by half. Add the stock, bring to the boil and then return the cutlets to the pan and simmer for a further 4–5 minutes.

Remove the cutlets from the pan and set aside to rest. Add the balsamic vinegar to the pan, then gradually whisk in the butter until the sauce is glossy. Season with salt and pepper. To serve, place a mound of spinach on each plate, top with a couple of cutlets and drizzle with some of the sauce. Serve with parmesan mash.

"Whisking in a little cold butter at the end will give the sauce a rich glossy finish."

CHOCOLATE HAZELNUT RICOTTA CAKE WITH CINNAMON POACHED FIGS

SERVES 6–8

100 G (3½ OZ) CASTER (SUPERFINE) SUGAR
2 TABLESPOONS PLAIN (ALL-PURPOSE) FLOUR
500 G (1 LB 2 OZ/2 CUPS) FRESH RICOTTA
1 TEASPOON VANILLA BEAN PASTE
2 TEASPOONS FINELY GRATED ORANGE ZEST
3 EGGS, LIGHTLY BEATEN
75 G (2¾ OZ) GOOD-QUALITY DARK CHOCOLATE, CHOPPED
75 G (2¾ OZ) HAZELNUTS, LIGHTLY TOASTED, SKINS REMOVED, CHOPPED

TO SERVE
CINNAMON POACHED FIGS, BELOW

Preheat the oven to 150°C (300°F/Gas 2). Butter and flour a 1 litre (35 fl oz/4 cup) loaf tin.

Mix together the sugar and flour. With electric beaters or in a mixer, beat the ricotta, vanilla and orange zest at low speed until smooth. Add the eggs, a little bit at a time, then add the sugar and flour and beat well. Stir in the chocolate and hazelnuts.

Pour the mixture into the tin and bake for 45 minutes, or until the cake is golden brown and a skewer poked into the middle comes out clean. (The cake will sink a little once it's removed from the oven.) Serve with the poached figs.

CINNAMON POACHED FIGS

SERVES 6–8

55 G (2 OZ/¼ CUP) CASTER (SUPERFINE) SUGAR
1 CINNAMON STICK
250 G (9 OZ) DRIED DESSERT FIGS, CHOPPED

Put the sugar and cinnamon in a saucepan over medium heat with 375 ml (13 fl oz/1½ cups) of water and stir to dissolve the sugar. Increase the heat to high and bring to the boil.

Add the figs to the syrup, return to the boil and then reduce the heat to low and simmer for 15 minutes, or until the figs are syrupy. Remove from the heat and leave to cool. Serve with the chocolate hazelnut ricotta cake.

CURRY NIGHT

LAMB BIRYANI

SERVES 4–6

1 KG (2 LB 4 OZ) BONELESS LAMB LEG, TRIMMED AND DICED
1 TABLESPOON GARAM MASALA
2 TEASPOONS GROUND CUMIN
1/2 TEASPOON TURMERIC
2 TABLESPOONS OLIVE OIL
1 ONION, THINLY SLICED
2 GARLIC CLOVES
2 TEASPOONS FINELY GRATED FRESH GINGER
300 G (10½ OZ/1½ CUPS) BASMATI RICE
750 ML (26 FL OZ/3 CUPS) CHICKEN STOCK
SMALL HANDFUL FRESH CORIANDER (CILANTRO) LEAVES

Preheat the oven to 200°C (400°F/Gas 6). Put the lamb in a large bowl with the garam masala, cumin and turmeric and toss to coat the lamb in the spices. Heat 1 tablespoon of the oil in a flameproof casserole over medium heat, add the lamb in batches and cook, stirring occasionally, for 3–4 minutes until browned all over, adding a little more oil if necessary. Remove and set aside.

Add the remaining oil, onion, garlic and ginger to the casserole and cook over medium heat until the onion is soft and pale golden. Add the rice, stir together and cook for 2 minutes. Return the lamb to the casserole in a single layer and carefully pour in the stock. Put the lid on the casserole and put in the oven. Cook for 35–45 minutes, or until the rice is tender and has absorbed all the liquid. Top with coriander leaves before serving.

CUMIN, MINT AND CORIANDER YOGHURT

SERVES 4–6

300 ML (10½ FL OZ) NATURAL YOGHURT
1 TEASPOON GROUND CUMIN
2 TABLESPOONS FINELY CHOPPED FRESH MINT
2 TABLESPOONS FINELY CHOPPED FRESH CORIANDER (CILANTRO)
2 CM (ABOUT 1 INCH) PIECE OF FRESH GINGER, PEELED AND GRATED
1 LONG GREEN CHILLI, SEEDED AND FINELY CHOPPED
SEA SALT
FRESHLY GROUND BLACK PEPPER
LIGHTLY TOASTED CUMIN SEEDS

Stir together the yoghurt, ground cumin, mint, coriander, ginger and chilli. Season well and sprinkle with cumin seeds. Serve as an accompaniment to curries.

FRAGRANT CHICKEN AND SPINACH CURRY

SERVES 4

2 TABLESPOONS VEGETABLE OIL
1 LARGE ONION, CHOPPED
2 TEASPOONS GROUND CUMIN
2 TEASPOONS GROUND CORIANDER
1/2 TEASPOON TURMERIC
PINCH OF CAYENNE PEPPER
2 GARLIC CLOVES, CRUSHED
1 TABLESPOON GRATED FRESH GINGER
750 G (1 LB 10 OZ) BONELESS CHICKEN THIGHS, CUBED
400 G (14 OZ) TIN CHOPPED TOMATOES
1/2 TEASPOON SEA SALT
2 TEASPOONS SOFT BROWN SUGAR
1 TABLESPOON LIME JUICE
90 G (3 1/4 OZ/2 CUPS) BABY ENGLISH SPINACH, FINELY CHOPPED
LARGE HANDFUL FRESH CORIANDER (CILANTRO) LEAVES, CHOPPED

TO SERVE
STEAMED RICE

Heat the oil in a large heavy-based pan over medium heat. Add the onion and cook, stirring, for 5–6 minutes until the onion is soft. Add the spices, garlic and ginger and cook, stirring, for 2 minutes more. Add the chicken and increase the heat to medium-high. Cook, stirring often, for 5 minutes, or until the chicken is browned.

Stir in the tomatoes and salt and bring to simmering point. Reduce the heat to low, cover the pan and simmer gently for 15 minutes. Add the sugar, lime juice and spinach and stir until the spinach has just wilted. Remove from the heat, sprinkle with coriander and serve with steamed rice.

"I've tried wine with Indian food, but nothing beats a cold beer, drunk straight from the bottle."

ALMOST-NO-COOKING DINNER FOR FRIENDS

CARAMEL SALMON

SERVES 4

1 TABLESPOON VEGETABLE OIL
800 G (1 LB 12 OZ) SALMON FILLETS, WITH SKIN, CUT INTO LARGE CUBES
1 RED ONION, SLICED
3 GARLIC CLOVES, SLICED
3 TABLESPOONS DARK SOY SAUCE
115 G (4 OZ/½ CUP) SOFT BROWN SUGAR
3 TABLESPOONS FISH SAUCE
FRESHLY GROUND BLACK PEPPER
1 TABLESPOON LIME JUICE

TO SERVE
STEAMED RICE
LIME WEDGES

Heat the oil in a large frying pan over high heat. Add the salmon in two batches and cook each batch for a couple of minutes until lightly browned. Turn over and cook the other side for 1 minute, then remove from the pan.

Reduce the heat to medium and add a little extra oil to the pan, if needed. Add the onion and garlic and cook for 3 minutes, stirring occasionally. Stir in the soy sauce, sugar and fish sauce. Return the salmon to the pan and cook for 1 minute, or until the sauce is rich, dark and syrupy. Sprinkle liberally with black pepper and stir through the lime juice.

Serve with steamed rice, with a little sauce drizzled over the top and lime wedges.

"This is my version of a traditional Vietnamese caramel dish."

CUCUMBER AND SNOW PEA SALAD

SERVES 4

1 LEBANESE (SHORT) CUCUMBER, THICKLY SLICED
150 G (5½ OZ) SNOW PEAS (MANGETOUT), TRIMMED, BLANCHED AND HALVED DIAGONALLY
2 TEASPOONS LIME JUICE
PINCH OF SUGAR
1 TABLESPOON OLIVE OIL

Put the cucumber and snow peas in a large bowl. Whisk together the lime juice, sugar and oil until the sugar dissolves. Pour over the cucumber and snow peas and toss well. Serve immediately.

FRESH FRUIT PLATE WITH LEMON GRASS SYRUP

SERVES 4

JUICE OF 1 ORANGE, STRAINED
JUICE OF 1 LEMON, STRAINED
JUICE OF 1 LIME, STRAINED
160 G (5¾ OZ) CASTER (SUPERFINE) SUGAR
2 LEMON GRASS STEMS, LIGHTLY CRUSHED AND CUT INTO 5 CM (2 INCH) LENGTHS
SELECTION OF SEASONAL FRUIT

Put the fruit juices, sugar and lemon grass in a saucepan over medium heat and stir to dissolve the sugar. Increase the heat to high and bring to the boil, then reduce the heat and leave to simmer for 10 minutes, or until slightly reduced and syrupy. Strain and leave to cool.

Choose a selection of fruit that is in season and at its best. Cut it up beautifully, arrange on a serving platter and drizzle with the lemon grass syrup

OK, so the downside of pretending it's the weekend on Thursday night is you have to get up and face Friday morning! But, if you had a few too many friday glasses of wine last night, it's probably nothing that a good honest BLT or croque madame can't cure.

Treat yourself to the best ingredients, like gruyère cheese, sourdough bread, roma tomatoes, freshly-sliced leg ham and organic bacon if you can find it. It's amazing the effect these will have on even the sorest head and the most jaded palate.

I'm lucky these days that I don't have to get up early and go to the markets like I used to. I remember when I was young and irresponsible I'd often have a couple of drinks after work with restaurant friends, which would quickly turn into a couple more, followed by pizza and wine. I'd stumble into bed at 11 pm on a Thursday night (it was always a Thursday) knowing I had to be up at 4 am to get to the markets. Sheer madness. Mind you, there was always a great Italian café waiting at the market to sort me out. Nothing fixes a hangover like a panini, a good coffee and just a few minutes to feel sorry for yourself. I suspect I'm a bit of a purist even where my hangovers are concerned.

If a good hangover is a great Australian tradition then another one is the barbie. I guess we're not the only nation on earth to have embraced the barbecue, but we're the only one to have made it part of our national culture. Guys have always loved cooking a barbecue, especially Australian guys, as long as it's outdoors and involves plenty of meat! Funnily enough, a new friend recently invited Natalie and me to her home for what we thought was going to be a good old Friday night barbie. "Come for a chop," she said, and we took her at her word, turning up in our most casual clothes and clutching an equally casual bottle of wine. Unfortunately the house was just about chock-full of Sydney's smartest and best-dressed, with not a chop in sight. So we learnt that, even in Australia, 'barbecue' can mean different things to different people. I think my favourite barbecue food falls somewhere in the middle of the two extremes. I still love the traditional great steaks or sausages, but I also like to experiment with things like quail or fish parcels stuffed full of amazing Asian flavours. There's almost no limit to what you can throw on the barbie!

I love Friday. I love the way you can feel the weekend creeping up on you, and there's a different kind of energy about people, knowing they don't have to work tomorrow. I often finish work a bit earlier and Friday night drinks are another great tradition, a symbolic start to the weekend. My days of hanging out at smart bars in the city might be over for a while, but there's nothing I like more than easing into the evening at home with Natalie, the girls, a few friends and, of course, a glass of wine or two while I fire up the barbie...

HANGOVER BREAKFASTS

CROQUE MADAME

SERVES 4

8 SLICES SOURDOUGH BREAD
BUTTER, TO SPREAD ON BREAD, PLUS 2 TEASPOONS EXTRA TO FRY EGGS
4 THICK SLICES LEG HAM
4 SLICES GRUYERE OR SWISS-STYLE CHEESE
SEA SALT
FRESHLY GROUND BLACK PEPPER
2 TABLESPOONS OLIVE OIL
4 EGGS
SHREDDED FLAT-LEAF (ITALIAN) PARSLEY

Spread four slices of bread with butter and top the unbuttered side with ham, cheese, salt and pepper and another slice of bread to make sandwiches. Butter the top of the sandwich, too.

Heat a large frying pan over medium heat. Add half the olive oil and swirl to cover the base of the pan. Put two sandwiches in the pan and put another heavy frying pan on top to squash them down. Cook for 1–2 minutes until they are golden underneath, then flip them over, replace the weight and cook for a couple of minutes more. Use the rest of the oil to cook the other two sandwiches. If you have a panini press, this is the time to use it, as an alternative to frying.

While the sandwiches are cooking, melt half the butter in a non-stick frying pan over medium heat. Crack 2 eggs into the pan, being careful not to break the yolks. Cook the eggs for about 2 minutes, or until just set. Wipe out the frying pan and fry the other 2 eggs in the remaining butter in the same way. Place a fried egg on each sandwich and sprinkle with shredded parsley.

"I used to have this at the first café I ever worked at — with a great dollop of mustard."

BREAKFAST BLT

MAKES 2

8 CHERRY TOMATOES, HALVED
4 SHORT-CUT BACON RASHERS
2 TEASPOONS OLIVE OIL
SEA SALT
FRESHLY GROUND BLACK PEPPER
1 AVOCADO
2 TABLESPOONS CREME FRAICHE
1 TABLESPOON LEMON JUICE
1 TABLESPOON SNIPPED CHIVES
DASH OF TABASCO SAUCE
4 SLICES SOURDOUGH BREAD
4 SMALL COS (ROMAINE) LETTUCE LEAVES

Preheat the oven to 200°C (400°F/Gas 6). Put the tomato halves and bacon on a baking tray lined with baking paper. Drizzle the tomatoes with the olive oil, season with salt and pepper and bake for 10 minutes, or until the bacon is crisp and tomatoes are slightly wilted.

Mash the avocado, crème fraiche, lemon juice and chives together and season with salt and pepper. Add Tabasco, to taste. Toast the bread and spread two of the slices with the avocado mixture. Top with lettuce leaves, some bacon and tomato halves and then sandwich with the other slices of bread.

"When I opened my own café, this is what I would make myself for breakfast."

FRIDAY DRINKS

CORN AND PRAWN FRITTERS

MAKES 24

125 G (4½ OZ/1 CUP) PLAIN (ALL-PURPOSE) FLOUR
1 TEASPOON BAKING POWDER
SEA SALT
4 SPRING ONIONS (SCALLIONS), THINLY SLICED
2 TABLESPOONS SNIPPED CHIVES
1 LONG GREEN CHILLI, SEEDED AND FINELY CHOPPED
185 ML (6 FL OZ/¾ CUP) SPARKLING MINERAL WATER
350 G (12 OZ) LARGE RAW PRAWNS (SHRIMP), PEELED, DEVEINED AND CHOPPED
200 G (7 OZ/1 CUP) FRESH CORN KERNELS
GREEN TABASCO SAUCE
1 EGG WHITE
OIL, FOR SHALLOW-FRYING
LEMON WEDGES

Sift the flour, baking powder and 1 teaspoon sea salt together in a large bowl. Add the spring onions, chives and chilli. Add the mineral water and fold together until just combined. Add the prawns, corn and a dash of Tabasco and stir together.

Beat the egg white until it forms stiff peaks. Carefully fold into the batter.

Heat the oil in a large frying pan over medium-high heat. For each fritter, drop 1 tablespoon of the batter into the hot oil and fry for 1–2 minutes on each side, or until golden brown. Drain on kitchen paper, sprinkle with sea salt and serve immediately with lemon wedges.

HAND-HELD PRAWNS

MAKES 20

4 TABLESPOONS OLIVE OIL
5 GARLIC CLOVES, CRUSHED
2 SMALL RED CHILLIES, SEEDED AND FINELY CHOPPED
2 TEASPOONS GRATED LEMON ZEST
2 TABLESPOONS CHOPPED FRESH FLAT-LEAF (ITALIAN) PARSLEY
20 LARGE RAW PRAWNS (SHRIMP), PEELED AND DEVEINED, TAILS LEFT INTACT

If you are using wooden skewers, soak them in water for a while beforehand so they don't scorch. Mix the olive oil, garlic, chilli, lemon zest and parsley in a large non-metallic bowl. Add the prawns and stir to coat them well, then cover the bowl and refrigerate for 30 minutes.

Preheat a chargrill pan or barbecue to high heat. Thread each prawn onto a skewer and cook for 2 minutes on each side, or until they are lightly charred and just cooked through.

CORIANDER-CRUMBED LAMB CUTLETS

MAKES 12

125 G (4½ OZ/1 CUP) PLAIN (ALL-PURPOSE) FLOUR
3 TABLESPOONS MILK
2 EGGS
160 G (5¾ OZ/2 CUPS) FRESH BREADCRUMBS
LARGE HANDFUL FRESH FLAT-LEAF (ITALIAN) PARSLEY, CHOPPED
2 TABLESPOONS FINELY CHOPPED FRESH CORIANDER (CILANTRO)
1 TEASPOON FINELY GRATED LEMON ZEST
1 TEASPOON GROUND CUMIN
SEA SALT
FRESHLY GROUND BLACK PEPPER
12 FRENCH-TRIMMED LAMB CUTLETS
125 ML (4 FL OZ/½ CUP) OLIVE OIL

TO SERVE
HERBED YOGHURT, BELOW

Put the flour in a flattish bowl. Lightly beat the milk and eggs in another bowl. Mix together the breadcrumbs, parsley, coriander, lemon zest and cumin in a third bowl and season with salt and pepper. Dip the lamb cutlets first in the flour, then in the beaten egg and finally in the breadcrumbs.

Heat the olive oil in a large frying pan over medium heat. Fry the cutlets, in batches so that you don't overcrowd the pan, for 2 minutes on each side until they are golden brown. Serve with herbed yoghurt.

HERBED YOGHURT

MAKES 125 ML (4 FL OZ/½ CUP)

125 ML (4 FL OZ/½ CUP) THICK GREEK YOGHURT
1 TEASPOON FINELY GRATED LEMON ZEST
1 TABLESPOON FINELY CHOPPED FRESH FLAT-LEAF (ITALIAN) PARSLEY
2 TABLESPOONS FINELY CHOPPED FRESH CORIANDER (CILANTRO)

Mix together all the ingredients and serve with the lamb cutlets.

HALF-SHELL SCALLOPS WITH GARLIC AND PARSLEY BREADCRUMBS

MAKES 16

50 G (1¾ OZ) BUTTER, SOFTENED
1 TABLESPOON EXTRA VIRGIN OLIVE OIL
1 FRENCH SHALLOT, FINELY DICED
2 TABLESPOONS FINELY CHOPPED MIXED FRESH HERBS
2 GARLIC CLOVES, CRUSHED
16 SCALLOPS ON THE SHELL
85 G (3 OZ/1 CUP) FRESH BREADCRUMBS
1 LEMON

Stir together the butter, olive oil, shallot, mixed herbs and garlic. Preheat the grill (broiler) to high. Spoon half a teaspoon of the herb butter over each scallop and sprinkle with some breadcrumbs. Grill until the butter has melted and the scallops are golden. Squeeze a little lemon juice over the top before handing around.

ZUCCHINI FRITTERS WITH MINT

SERVES 8

500 G (1 LB 2 OZ) ZUCCHINI (COURGETTES), TRIMMED
30 G (1 OZ/¼ CUP) PLAIN (ALL-PURPOSE) FLOUR
SEA SALT
FRESHLY GROUND BLACK PEPPER
2 TABLESPOONS OLIVE OIL, PLUS EXTRA TO DRIZZLE
1 TABLESPOON RED WINE VINEGAR
2 TABLESPOONS FINELY SHREDDED FRESH MINT

Cut the zucchini on the diagonal into 5 mm (¼ inch) thick slices. Put the flour in a bowl and season well. Toss the zucchini in the seasoned flour.

Heat the olive oil in a large non-stick frying pan over medium-high heat. Add the zucchini, in batches if necessary, and fry for 2 minutes on each side until golden brown, adding more oil if needed. Drain on kitchen paper.

Put the zucchini in a serving dish, sprinkle with the red wine vinegar and scatter with mint. Drizzle with a little extra olive oil and serve immediately.

SPICED PEPITAS

MAKES 150 G (5½ OZ/1 CUP)

150 G (5½ OZ/1 CUP) PEPITAS (PUMPKIN SEEDS)
2 TEASPOONS EXTRA VIRGIN OLIVE OIL
1 TEASPOON PAPRIKA
½ TEASPOON SPANISH SWEET SMOKED PAPRIKA
PINCH OF CAYENNE PEPPER
SEA SALT

Preheat the oven to 180°C (350°F/Gas 4). Line a large baking tray with baking paper, spread the pepitas out on the tray and roast for 12 minutes, or until lightly toasted.

Put the pepitas in a large bowl, add the olive oil and toss together. Add the spices and toss again. Season with sea salt.

SWEETCORN BLINIS WITH CREME FRAICHE AND SALMON ROE

MAKES ABOUT 30

500 G (1 LB 2 OZ) CORN KERNELS, CUT FROM 3 LARGE CORN COBS
2 EGGS
125 G (4½ OZ/1 CUP) PLAIN (ALL-PURPOSE) FLOUR
1 TEASPOON BAKING POWDER
SEA SALT
PINCH OF WHITE PEPPER
BUTTER, FOR GREASING THE PAN
2 SPRING ONIONS (SCALLIONS), FINELY SLICED
150 ML (5 FL OZ) CREME FRAICHE
100 G (3½ OZ) SALMON ROE

Preheat the oven to 120°C (235°F/Gas ½). Put the corn, eggs, flour, baking powder, salt and pepper in a blender or processor and mix until almost smooth.

Heat a frying pan over medium-high heat and brush with butter. For each blini, drop 1 tablespoon of mixture into the pan, sprinkle with one or two slices of spring onion and cook in batches of about six for 1 minute each side. Drain on paper towels and keep warm in the oven while you cook the rest.

Arrange the blinis on a serving platter and top each one with a teaspoon of crème fraiche and a little salmon roe.

WATERMELON VODKA

MAKES 4

160 ML (5¼ FL OZ) VODKA
ABOUT ¼ SMALL WATERMELON, CHOPPED
1 CUP ICE CUBES

Put all the ingredients in a blender and mix until smooth.

POMEGRANATE JUICE WITH PROSECCO

MAKES 6

250 ML (9 FL OZ/1 CUP) POMEGRANATE JUICE
750 ML (26 FL OZ/3 CUPS) PROSECCO

Pour the pomegranate juice into six champagne flutes. Top with the prosecco.

"I never bother to assemble the blinis unless it's a formal do. I just put the salmon roe and crème fraiche in little bowls and let my friends serve themselves."

"Pepitas are simply pumpkin seeds, and they make a delicious alternative to the usual party nuts."

"It's easy now
to buy quails
partially boned
and butterflied,
which makes
them super-
convenient for
barbecuing."

"COME OVER FOR A CHOP!"

BARBIE NUMBER ONE

BARBECUED QUAIL WITH SPICED SALT AND LEMON

SERVES 4

6 X 150–200 G (5–7 OZ) QUAIL
1 TABLESPOON SESAME SEEDS
2 TEASPOONS GROUND CUMIN
SEA SALT
2 TABLESPOONS EXTRA VIRGIN OLIVE OIL
FRESHLY GROUND BLACK PEPPER

TO SERVE
LEMON WEDGES

Cut each quail through the breastbone with a sharp knife and flatten out with the palm of your hand. Cut down either side of the backbone and remove.

Put the sesame seeds, cumin and 2 teaspoons sea salt in a small frying pan over medium heat. Cook, stirring, for 1–2 minutes, or until the sesame seeds are lightly toasted and fragrant.

Preheat a barbecue chargrill plate to high. Brush each quail with olive oil and season with salt and pepper. Cook the quail, skin-side-down, on the chargrill for 5 minutes each side, or until crisp and cooked through. Serve the quail with a sprinkling of spiced salt and a squeeze of lemon.

RICE, BROAD BEAN AND ARTICHOKE SALAD

SERVES 4

220 G (7¾ OZ/1 CUP) SHORT-GRAIN RICE
3 TABLESPOONS EXTRA VIRGIN OLIVE OIL
2 TABLESPOONS LEMON JUICE
SEA SALT
FRESHLY GROUND BLACK PEPPER
3 TABLESPOONS FINELY CHOPPED FRESH PARSLEY
185 G (6½ OZ/1 CUP) PEELED, BLANCHED AND SKINNED BROAD (FAVA) BEANS
FRESH MINT LEAVES
6 MARINATED ARTICHOKE HEARTS, QUARTERED

Cook the rice in a large pan of salted boiling water until it is cooked but still has a little 'bite', and then drain. Put the rice in a mixing bowl with the olive oil, lemon juice, salt and pepper and mix together. Leave to cool. Add the parsley, beans, mint leaves and artichoke hearts and stir together.

BARBIE NUMBER TWO

FRAGRANT FISH PARCELS

SERVES 4

4 X 150 G (5½ OZ) FIRM WHITE FISH FILLETS (SUCH AS COD, SNAPPER OR LING)
80 ML (2½ FL OZ/⅓ CUP) COCONUT MILK
2 TEASPOONS LIME JUICE
2 TEASPOONS FISH SAUCE
1 TEASPOON SOFT BROWN SUGAR
1 LEMON GRASS STEM, OUTER LAYERS REMOVED, BRUISED AND THINLY SLICED
2 MAKRUT (KAFFIR LIME) LEAVES, CENTRE VEINS REMOVED, VERY THINLY SLICED
SMALL HANDFUL FRESH CORIANDER (CILANTRO) LEAVES
SMALL HANDFUL FRESH THAI BASIL LEAVES

TO SERVE
LIME WEDGES

Preheat a barbecue or chargrill plate to hot. Put each fish fillet on a 30 cm (12 inch) long piece of foil.

Mix together the coconut milk, lime juice, fish sauce and sugar and spoon over the fish fillets. Scatter the lemon grass, makrut leaves, coriander and Thai basil over the fish.

Fold in the sides of the foil to make parcels. Cook on the barbecue or chargrill for 5–10 minutes, depending upon the thickness of your fish — the fish should be just cooked through. Serve with lime wedges.

"When you open these parcels, you're greeted by the most incredible aroma — it's irresistible."

PINK GRAPEFRUIT, BEAN AND CASHEW SALAD WITH LIME DRESSING

SERVES 4

1 LARGE RUBY GRAPEFRUIT
400 G (14 OZ) GREEN BEANS, TOPPED BUT NOT TAILED
3 TABLESPOONS CASHEW NUTS
LARGE HANDFUL FRESH CORIANDER (CILANTRO) LEAVES
3 SPRING ONIONS (SCALLIONS), SLICED ON THE DIAGONAL
LIME DRESSING, BELOW

Peel the grapefruit by slicing off both ends. Stand the end of the fruit on a board and, following the curve of the grapefruit, slice off all the peel and pith with a sharp knife. Slice out segments of the grapefruit by cutting between the membrane.

Blanch the beans in boiling water for 1–2 minutes until just tender. Refresh under cold water.

Heat a frying pan over high heat and cook the cashews, stirring, for 2–3 minutes until lightly roasted. Roughly chop the nuts and set aside. Toss the grapefruit, beans, coriander and spring onions with the dressing. Arrange on a large serving plate and sprinkle with the roasted cashews before serving.

LIME DRESSING

30 ML (1 FL OZ) FISH SAUCE
30 ML (1 FL OZ) LIME JUICE
1 TABLESPOON SOFT BROWN SUGAR
1 SMALL RED CHILLI, FINELY CHOPPED

Stir together all the ingredients until the sugar has dissolved.

BARBIE NUMBER THREE

SAUSAGES WITH STEWED PEPPERS

SERVES 6

3 RED PEPPERS (CAPSICUMS), SEEDED AND CUT INTO THICK STRIPS
2 GARLIC CLOVES, THINLY SLICED
3 TABLESPOONS RED WINE VINEGAR
1/2 TEASPOON SEA SALT
2 TEASPOONS SOFT BROWN SUGAR
2 TABLESPOONS EXTRA VIRGIN OLIVE OIL
FRESHLY GROUND BLACK PEPPER
1 TABLESPOON SHREDDED FRESH FLAT-LEAF (ITALIAN) PARSLEY
24 CHIPOLATA SAUSAGES

Put the peppers, garlic, vinegar, salt, sugar and 1 tablespoon of the oil in a frying pan over medium heat and cook, covered, for 25 minutes, stirring occasionally, until the peppers are soft. Season with black pepper. Spoon into a serving dish, leave to cool and then drizzle with the rest of the olive oil and sprinkle with parsley. Meanwhile, barbecue the sausages and then serve with the peppers.

RADICCHIO SLAW

SERVES 6

2 HEADS OF RADICCHIO, OUTER LEAVES TRIMMED, FINELY SHREDDED
1 RED ONION, THINLY SLICED
2 TABLESPOONS CHOPPED FRESH FLAT-LEAF (ITALIAN) PARSLEY
1 1/2 TABLESPOONS OLIVE OIL
2 TABLESPOONS LEMON JUICE
SEA SALT
FRESHLY GROUND BLACK PEPPER

Stir together the radicchio, onion and parsley. Whisk together the oil, lemon juice, salt and pepper and pour over the salad. Toss together well.

ROSEMARY AND OLIVE SPELT BREAD

SERVES 8

250 G (9 OZ/2 CUPS) SPELT FLOUR
250 G (9 OZ/2 CUPS) PLAIN (ALL-PURPOSE) FLOUR
1 TEASPOON HONEY
300 ML (10½ FL OZ) TEPID WATER
7 G (¼ OZ) INSTANT DRIED YEAST
3 TABLESPOONS OLIVE OIL
SEA SALT
ROSEMARY SPRIGS AND PITTED OLIVES, TO DECORATE

Sift the spelt and plain flours together into a large bowl. Put about ½ cupful of the combined flours into a smaller bowl with the honey and water and whisk to combine. Sprinkle the yeast over the top, whisk again and set aside for 10 minutes for the yeast to activate. Bubbles should appear on the surface of the mixture.

Add the oil and 2 teaspoons of salt to the bowl of flour. Make a well in the centre and pour in the yeast mixture. Mix to form a soft but firm dough. Transfer to a lightly floured work surface and knead for about 10 minutes until the dough is smooth, elastic and shiny. Put the dough in a clean, lightly oiled bowl, cover with plastic wrap and leave to rise in a warm place for an hour, or until it has doubled in size.

Knock the dough back by punching it with your fist, then leave it to rest for 5 minutes. Sit the dough on a large, lightly oiled baking tray and stretch it out as far as you can to make a rough rectangle.

Cover the dough and set aside for a further 30 minutes. Preheat the oven to 220°C (425°F/Gas 7). Poke holes all over the dough with your thumb. Push rosemary sprigs and olives into the holes and brush the top with a little olive oil. Sprinkle the bread with extra sea salt.

Bake for 10 minutes, then reduce the heat to 190°C (375°F/Gas 5) and bake for a further 12–15 minutes until golden brown and risen.

"Spelt is an ancient variety of wheat. It's packed with flavour and is enjoying renewed popularity."

"This is really just a grown-up version of a sausage in a bread roll with tomato sauce."

PAVLOVA WITH YOGHURT CREAM AND STRAWBERRIES

SERVES 8

6 EGG WHITES
1/4 TEASPOON CREAM OF TARTAR
1 TEASPOON NATURAL VANILLA EXTRACT
300 G (10½ OZ/1⅓ CUPS) CASTER (SUPERFINE) SUGAR
1 TABLESPOON CORNFLOUR (CORNSTARCH)
2 TABLESPOONS ARROWROOT
2 TEASPOONS WHITE VINEGAR

TO SERVE
250 ML (9 FL OZ/1 CUP) CREAM, WHIPPED
125 ML (4 FL OZ/½ CUP) NATURAL YOGHURT
250 G (9 OZ) STRAWBERRIES, HULLED AND HALVED, IF LARGE
1 TABLESPOON ICING (CONFECTIONERS') SUGAR

Preheat the oven to 180°C (350°F/Gas 4) and line a baking tray with baking paper. Draw a circle on the paper about 20 cm (8 inches) in diameter.

Beat the egg whites, cream of tartar and vanilla in a clean dry bowl until stiff peaks form. Add the sugar a tablespoon at a time, beating continuously until the meringue is glossy and thick. Stir in the cornflour, arrowroot and vinegar.

Pile the meringue onto the circle on the baking tray and put in the oven. Immediately reduce the oven to 120°C (235°F/Gas ½) and bake the pavlova for 1 hour 20 minutes, or until the outside is firm but not browned. Turn off the oven and leave the pavlova inside, with the door ajar, until completely cooled.

Gently fold together the cream and yoghurt. Toss the strawberries with the icing sugar. Spoon the yoghurt cream over the pavlova and top with strawberries to serve.

"Pavs are a great antipodean tradition — the yoghurt cream is my little twist."

Saturday is food shopping day. saturday I love the satisfaction that comes from a full weekend fridge and I try to shop in the 'old-fashioned' way — greengrocer for vegies, butcher for meat, so that it's a social pleasure. I get far too stressed-out fighting for a space in the supermarket carpark.

I usually make a special breakfast on Saturday morning and then we'll go out for coffee (even the worst café makes better coffee than I do at home) and do our weekly shopping. Some weekends we'll go to the amazing fish markets here in Sydney. I didn't eat fish until I moved to Sydney — with Dad being a butcher we just grew up on so much meat! Now I love the bustle and excitement of the fish markets, watching the bidding and buying special Saturday lunchtime treats. Sometimes we'll rush home and make up a decadent shellfish plate with freshly-shucked oysters, lobster tails and Balmain bugs, and a couple of quick dressings for dipping.

I'm an active person by nature, but in the middle of a Sydney winter, or even on a wet summer Saturday, I love to switch on the lamps and snuggle in. Just staying indoors can feel like a real treat. Some families like to play Scrabble, read books, watch movies, but without a doubt our favourite family pastime on a rainy Saturday is baking. To stop us all going stir-crazy the mixer comes out and we'll start chopping and whizzing, filling the house with the smell of butter, sugar and vanilla, and the sound of eggs cracking. The girls all sit up on the kitchen bench and become very competitive over who does what. We generally have to

CHORIZO, POTATO AND RED PEPPER FRITTATA

SERVES 4

1½ TABLESPOONS OLIVE OIL
1 CHORIZO SAUSAGE, SLICED
1 RED-SKINNED POTATO, DICED
1 SMALL ONION, DICED
1 RED PEPPER (CAPSICUM), DICED
10 EGGS
2 TABLESPOONS CHOPPED FRESH FLAT-LEAF (ITALIAN) PARSLEY
2 TABLESPOONS FINELY GRATED PARMESAN CHEESE

Heat 2 teaspoons of the oil in a 20 cm (8 inch) frying pan over medium-high heat and cook the chorizo, stirring occasionally, for 5–6 minutes, or until crisp. Drain on kitchen paper.

Turn the heat to medium, add the remaining oil, the potato and onion to the pan and cook, stirring occasionally, for 5 minutes, or until the onion is soft. Add the pepper and cook for 5 minutes before returning the chorizo to the pan. Preheat your grill (broiler) to hot.

Whisk the eggs and pour into the pan. Reduce the heat to low, cover the pan and cook until the eggs have almost set. Sprinkle with parsley and parmesan and then put under the grill for 3–4 minutes until the frittata is golden and puffed.

"Serve this with soft bread rolls, bitter green leaves and a good store-bought tomato chutney."

FISHMARKET LUNCH

SHELLFISH PLATE WITH SHALLOT VINAIGRETTE AND COCKTAIL SAUCE

Arrange a selection of fresh seafood on a platter and serve with shallot vinaigrette and cocktail sauce. I like to use freshly shucked oysters, Balmain bug tails and king prawns (shrimp).

SHALLOT VINAIGRETTE

2 FRENCH SHALLOTS, FINELY CHOPPED
3 TABLESPOONS GRAPESEED OIL
2 TABLESPOONS RICE VINEGAR
1 TEASPOON GRATED FRESH GINGER
2 TEASPOONS LIME JUICE
1 TEASPOON SESAME OIL
1 TEASPOON SOFT BROWN SUGAR

Mix all the ingredients together in a small bowl, stirring to dissolve the sugar.

COCKTAIL SAUCE

125 ML (4 FL OZ/$\frac{1}{2}$ CUP) MAYONNAISE
2 TABLESPOONS TOMATO SAUCE
1 TABLESPOON WORCESTERSHIRE SAUCE
1 TABLESPOON LEMON JUICE
A DASH OF TABASCO SAUCE

Stir all the ingredients together in a small bowl.

BAKING

LEMON POUND CAKE

SERVES 12–16

250 G (9 OZ) UNSALTED BUTTER, SOFTENED
250 G (9 OZ) CASTER (SUPERFINE) SUGAR
2 TEASPOONS FINELY GRATED LEMON ZEST
1 TEASPOON NATURAL VANILLA EXTRACT
4 EGGS
250 G (9 OZ/2 CUPS) SELF-RAISING FLOUR, SIFTED
LEMON BUTTER ICING, BELOW

Preheat the oven to 180°C (350°F/Gas 4). Grease and line the base of a deep 20 cm (8 inch) square baking tin with baking paper.

Beat the butter and sugar with electric beaters until pale and creamy. Beat in the lemon zest and vanilla. Add the eggs one at a time, beating until just combined after each addition. Fold in the sifted flour in two batches until well combined.

Spoon into the tin and bake for 40–50 minutes, or until a skewer poked into the middle of the cake comes out clean. Cover loosely with foil if browning too quickly. Cool for 10 minutes before removing from the tin and turning out onto a wire rack to cool completely. Ice with lemon butter icing, below.

LEMON BUTTER ICING

3 TABLESPOONS UNSALTED BUTTER
110 G (3¾ OZ) ICING (CONFECTIONERS') SUGAR, SIFTED
2 TEASPOONS FINELY GRATED LEMON ZEST
2 TEASPOONS LEMON JUICE

Beat the butter with electric beaters until very soft and white. Beat in the icing sugar, lemon zest and juice. Spread over the cake.

RASPBERRY TARTS

MAKES 12

220 G (7¾ OZ/1 CUP) CASTER (SUPERFINE) SUGAR
300 G (10½ OZ) FRESH RASPBERRIES
250 G (9 OZ/2 CUPS) PLAIN (ALL-PURPOSE) FLOUR
125 G (4½ OZ) ICING (CONFECTIONERS') SUGAR
A PINCH OF SALT
180 G (6½ OZ) UNSALTED BUTTER, CHILLED AND CUBED
60 ML (2 FL OZ/¼ CUP) ICED WATER
185 G (6½ OZ/¾ CUP) MASCARPONE CHEESE
185 ML (6 FL OZ/¾ CUP) CREAM, LIGHTLY WHIPPED
1 TEASPOON VANILLA BEAN PASTE

To make a raspberry syrup, put the caster sugar in a pan with 60 ml (2 fl oz/¼ cup) of water and stir over low heat to dissolve the sugar. Increase the heat and bring to the boil. Cook until golden, then remove from the heat. Mash 100 g (3½ oz) of the raspberries and stir into the syrup. Leave to cool.

Sift the flour, icing sugar and salt in a bowl and stir to combine. Using your fingertips, rub in the butter until the mixture resembles coarse breadcrumbs. Add the iced water and mix until the dough comes together in a ball. Wrap in plastic wrap and chill for 30 minutes. Roll out on a lightly floured surface until 3 mm (⅛ inch) thick, then press lightly into 12 individual tart tins and prick with a fork. Chill for 30 minutes.

Preheat the oven to 200°C (400°F/Gas 6). Line the chilled pastry with baking paper and add baking weights or uncooked rice. Bake for 10 minutes, then remove the paper and weights. Bake for another 10 minutes, or until the pastry is golden and crisp. Leave to cool.

Remove the pastry cases from the tins and arrange on a serving plate. Mix together the mascarpone, cream and vanilla bean paste and spoon into the cases. Arrange the rest of the raspberries on top and drizzle with the raspberry syrup.

LAMINGTONS

MAKES 16

SPONGE CAKE
6 EGGS
150 G (5$\frac{1}{2}$ OZ/$^2/_3$ CUP) CASTER (SUPERFINE) SUGAR
200 G (7 OZ/1$^2/_3$ CUPS) SELF-RAISING FLOUR
30 G (1 OZ) UNSALTED BUTTER, MELTED

CHOCOLATE ICING
500 G (1 LB 2 OZ/4 CUPS) ICING (CONFECTIONERS') SUGAR
200 G (7 OZ) DARK CHOCOLATE, CHOPPED
15 G ($^1/_2$ OZ) UNSALTED BUTTER
125 ML (4 FL OZ/$^1/_2$ CUP) MILK
375 G (13 OZ/4 CUPS) DESICCATED COCONUT

Preheat the oven to 180°C (350°F/Gas 4). Lightly grease and line the base of an 18 x 28 cm (7 x 11 inch) tin with baking paper.

To make the cake, beat the eggs for about 5 minutes with an electric mixer until light and fluffy. Gradually add the sugar and continue beating until the mixture is thick and the sugar has dissolved. Sift in the flour and fold in lightly. Add the butter and 3 tablespoons of hot water and stir gently to combine. Pour into the tin and bake for 30 minutes, or until golden. Cool on a wire rack.

To make the chocolate icing, put the sugar, dark chocolate, butter and milk in a heatproof bowl and place over a saucepan of simmering water. Stir constantly until melted and mixed together.

Cut the sponge into 16 squares. Put the coconut in a bowl. Dip each sponge square into the chocolate icing and then in the coconut. Leave on a wire rack to dry completely before serving.

FRESH APRICOT AND CINNAMON CAKE

SERVES 8

140 G (5 OZ) SELF-RAISING FLOUR
1/2 TEASPOON GROUND CINNAMON
50 G (1¾ OZ/¼ CUP) CASTER (SUPERFINE) SUGAR
1 EGG, LIGHTLY BEATEN
3 TABLESPOONS MILK
1 TEASPOON NATURAL VANILLA EXTRACT
85 G (3 OZ) UNSALTED BUTTER, MELTED
350 G (12 OZ) FRESH APRICOTS, HALVED AND PITTED

TOPPING
40 G (1½ OZ/⅓ CUP) PLAIN (ALL-PURPOSE) FLOUR
1 TEASPOON GROUND CINNAMON
35 G (1¼ OZ) CASTER (SUPERFINE) SUGAR
35 G (1¼ OZ) UNSALTED BUTTER, CHILLED AND DICED

Preheat the oven to 180°C (350°F/Gas 4). Grease and line the base of a 20 cm (8 inch) round spring-form tin. Sift the flour and cinnamon into a large bowl and stir in the sugar. Make a well in the centre and pour in the egg, milk, vanilla and melted butter. Mix with a wooden spoon until the batter is smooth, then spoon into the tin. Arrange the apricots, cut-side-up, evenly over the batter and then gently press them down.

For the topping, put the flour, cinnamon and sugar in a bowl. Rub in the butter with your fingertips until crumbs form. Scatter the topping evenly over the apricots.

Bake for 35–40 minutes, or until the cake is light golden and a skewer poked into the middle comes out clean. Leave to cool in the tin for 10 minutes before transferring to a wire rack to cool completely.

"At my school we'd have lamington drives to raise money. They got incredibly competitive!"

DINNER PARTIES

CHINESE MEMORIES

LEMON CHICKEN

SERVES 4

2 TABLESPOONS PLAIN (ALL-PURPOSE) FLOUR
1 TEASPOON CHINESE FIVE-SPICE
SEA SALT
FRESHLY GROUND BLACK PEPPER
4 X 180 G (6½ OZ) BONELESS CHICKEN BREASTS WITH SKIN
VEGETABLE OIL, FOR SHALLOW-FRYING
1 LEMON, CUT INTO WEDGES
3 CM (1 INCH) PIECE OF FRESH GINGER, PEELED AND CUT INTO THIN STRIPS
4 TABLESPOONS HONEY
2 TABLESPOONS CHINESE RICE WINE
80 ML (2½ FL OZ/⅓ CUP) LEMON JUICE
2 TABLESPOONS LIGHT SOY SAUCE
80 ML (2½ FL OZ/⅓ CUP) CHICKEN STOCK
2 TABLESPOONS SOFT BROWN SUGAR
2 TEASPOONS CORNFLOUR (CORNSTARCH), MIXED WITH A LITTLE COLD WATER

Preheat the oven to 180°C (350°F/Gas 4). Mix the flour, five-spice, salt and pepper on a large plate. Dust the chicken in the spiced flour.

Heat enough oil for shallow-frying in a large wok over medium-high heat. Fry the chicken breasts for 2–3 minutes, or until the skin is crisp and golden. Drain on kitchen paper, then put the chicken on a baking tray and bake for 6 minutes, or until just cooked through.

Meanwhile, drain all but 2 tablespoons of the oil from the wok and return to high heat. Add the lemon wedges and ginger and stir-fry for 2 minutes. Add the honey, rice wine and lemon juice and cook for 1 minute, then add the soy sauce, chicken stock and sugar and simmer for 2 minutes. Add the cornflour mixture and simmer for 2 minutes, or until slightly thickened. Remove from the heat.

To serve, cut each chicken breast into five or six pieces and spoon some sauce over the top.

CHILLI AND GARLIC PRAWNS WITH ASPARAGUS

SERVES 4

2 TABLESPOONS PEANUT OIL
24 RAW KING PRAWNS (SHRIMP), PEELED AND DEVEINED, TAILS LEFT INTACT
1 ONION, CUT INTO THIN WEDGES
2 LONG RED CHILLIES, SEEDED AND FINELY CHOPPED
2 GARLIC CLOVES, FINELY CHOPPED
350 G (12 OZ/2 BUNCHES) ASPARAGUS, TRIMMED AND CUT INTO LONG LENGTHS
1 TABLESPOON CHINESE RICE WINE
1 TABLESPOON LIGHT SOY SAUCE
PINCH OF CASTER (SUPERFINE) SUGAR

Heat 1 tablespoon of the oil in a large wok over high heat. Add the prawns and stir-fry for 2–3 minutes, or until just cooked through. Remove from the wok and set aside.

Add the remaining oil and the onion to the wok and stir-fry for 1–2 minutes, or until golden. Add the chilli and garlic and stir-fry for 30 seconds. Add the asparagus and stir-fry for 2 minutes, or until just tender. Add the rice wine, soy sauce and sugar and toss together. Return the prawns to the wok and cook for 1 minute to heat through. Serve immediately.

BAKED CHINESE RICE WITH PEAS AND GINGER

SERVES 4

1 TABLESPOON PEANUT OIL
500 G (1 LB 2 OZ) CHINESE CABBAGE, CUT INTO 1 CM (½ INCH) THICK SLICES
3 CM (ABOUT 1 INCH) PIECE OF FRESH GINGER, PEELED AND JULIENNED
SEA SALT
1 TABLESPOON CHINESE RICE WINE
220 G (7¾ OZ/1 CUP) SHORT-GRAIN RICE, RINSED
130 G (4½ OZ/1 CUP) FROZEN BABY PEAS, THAWED
SMALL HANDFUL FRESH CORIANDER (CILANTRO) LEAVES

Preheat the oven to 180°C (350°F/Gas 4). Heat the oil in a large flameproof casserole. Add the cabbage and ginger and cook, stirring, for 1–2 minutes until the cabbage has just wilted. Season with sea salt, add the Chinese rice wine and toss together.

Add the rice and toss to coat in the oil. Add 435 ml (15 fl oz/1¾ cups) of cold water, bring to the boil and then cover and put in the oven for 20 minutes. Remove from the oven, stir through the peas, then cover again and set aside to steam for a further 10 minutes.

To serve, fluff the rice with a fork or chopsticks and sprinkle with the coriander.

LITTLE STEAMED GINGER PUDDINGS WITH COCONUT CUSTARD

MAKES 4

100 G (3½ OZ) UNSALTED BUTTER, SOFTENED
100 G (3½ OZ) CASTER (SUPERFINE) SUGAR
2 EGGS, LIGHTLY BEATEN
125 G (4½ OZ) CRYSTALLIZED GINGER, FINELY CHOPPED
125 G (4½ OZ/1 CUP) SELF-RAISING FLOUR
150 ML (5 FL OZ) MILK

TO SERVE
COCONUT CUSTARD, BELOW
CRYSTALLIZED GINGER

Lightly butter four 250 ml (9 fl oz/1 cup) pudding basins.

Cream the butter and sugar together until pale and creamy. Add the eggs a little at a time, beating well after each addition. Stir through the ginger. Fold in spoonfuls of sifted flour, alternating with spoonfuls of milk until both are added and you have a smooth batter. Spoon into the pudding basins.

Cut four pieces of baking paper and fold a thin pleat down the middle of each one. Place a piece over each basin and tie with string. Put the puddings in a steamer over a saucepan of gently simmering water and steam for 40 minutes, or until cooked through. Check the water level in the saucepan from time to time. Turn out and serve with coconut custard and a sprinkling of crystallized ginger.

COCONUT CUSTARD

SERVES 4

400 ML (14 FL OZ) COCONUT CREAM
2 EGG YOLKS
2 TABLESPOONS CASTER (SUPERFINE) SUGAR
1 TEASPOON CORNFLOUR (CORNSTARCH)

Put all the ingredients in a small pan and whisk together. Stir, without boiling, over low heat for 5–10 minutes until the custard has thickened enough to coat the back of your wooden spoon.

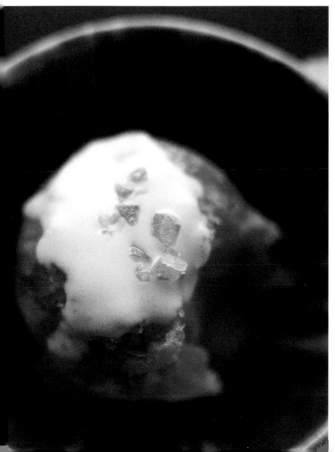

"This is my 21st century take on childhood memories of Chinese dining in suburban Melbourne."

SUMMER DINNER PARTY

RICOTTA- AND HERB-STUFFED ROAST CHICKEN

SERVES 4

1.6 KG (3 LB 8 OZ) FREE-RANGE CHICKEN
375 G (13 OZ/1½ CUPS) FRESH RICOTTA
2 TABLESPOONS SNIPPED CHIVES
2 TABLESPOONS CHOPPED FRESH CHERVIL
2 TEASPOONS GRATED LEMON ZEST
SEA SALT
FRESHLY GROUND BLACK PEPPER
OLIVE OIL

Preheat the oven to 200°C (400°F/Gas 6). To spatchcock the chicken, place the bird, breast-side-down, on a board. Using poultry shears or a sharp knife, cut along both sides of the backbone, cutting through the skin and bone. Remove the backbone. Turn the bird over and press firmly on the breast bone to break the bone and flatten the breast. Tuck the wing tips under the breast.

Mix together the ricotta, herbs, lemon zest, salt and pepper. With your fingers, carefully loosen the skin over the breast of the chicken and down to the thigh area. Spread the ricotta mixture evenly under the skin to cover the breast and thigh.

Put the chicken in a roasting tin, drizzle with olive oil and season with salt and pepper. Roast for 50 minutes, or until the juices run clear when you poke a skewer into the thickest part of the thigh. Leave to rest for 5 minutes before carving.

CORN WITH FRENCH BEANS

SERVES 4

1 TABLESPOON OLIVE OIL
1 TABLESPOON BUTTER
3 SPRING ONIONS (SCALLIONS), THINLY SLICED
1 GARLIC CLOVE, CRUSHED
400 G (14 OZ/2 CUPS) CORN KERNELS, CUT FROM THE COB
250 G (9 OZ) GREEN BEANS, TOPPED
125 ML (4 FL OZ/½ CUP) CHICKEN STOCK
SEA SALT
FRESHLY GROUND BLACK PEPPER

Heat the oil and butter in a large pan over medium heat. When the butter has melted, add the spring onions and cook, stirring occasionally, for 1–2 minutes until they are soft. Add the garlic and cook, stirring, for another minute. Add the corn and beans and cook, stirring occasionally, for 2–3 minutes, then add the chicken stock. Cover the pan and cook for a further 3–4 minutes until the beans are bright green and crisply tender. Season and serve.

RASPBERRY, PISTACHIO AND ROSEWATER SEMIFREDDO

SERVES 6–8

6 EGG YOLKS
3 TABLESPOONS HONEY
250 ML (9 FL OZ/1 CUP) CREAM, WHIPPED
2 TEASPOONS ROSEWATER
150 G (5½ OZ) FRESH RASPBERRIES, PLUS A FEW EXTRA TO SERVE
3 TABLESPOONS SHELLED PISTACHIO NUTS, CHOPPED

Beat the egg yolks and honey together with electric beaters for 10 minutes, or until thick, pale, creamy and doubled in volume. Fold in the whipped cream and rosewater until just combined.

Line the base and two sides of a 1 litre (35 fl oz/4 cup) loaf tin with a piece of plastic wrap, leaving the wrap hanging over the sides of the tin. Spoon the mixture into the tin, fold the plastic over the top to cover the semifreddo and freeze for 1–2 hours, or until partially frozen. Remove from the freezer and stir through the raspberries and pistachios. Cover with plastic wrap and return to the freezer until completely frozen.

Before serving, leave to soften in the fridge for 20 minutes. Turn out of the tin, cut into slices and serve with a few extra raspberries.

PAELLA PARTY

PAELLA

SERVES 6

80 ML (2½ FL OZ/⅓ CUP) OLIVE OIL
1 CHORIZO SAUSAGE, THINLY SLICED
200 G (7 OZ) FRENCH SHALLOTS, SLICED
SEA SALT
2 GARLIC CLOVES, CRUSHED
2 TEASPOONS SWEET PAPRIKA
¼ TEASPOON CAYENNE PEPPER
500 G (1 LB 2 OZ) SPANISH CALASPARRA RICE (OR USE ARBORIO)
400 G (14 OZ) TIN CHOPPED TOMATOES
½ TEASPOON SAFFRON, SOAKED IN 1 TABLESPOON WATER
1 RED PEPPER (CAPSICUM), ROASTED, PEELED AND THINLY SLICED
1.25 LITRES (44 FL OZ/5 CUPS) CHICKEN STOCK
300 G (10½ OZ) GREEN BEANS, CHOPPED
18 LARGE RAW PRAWNS (SHRIMP), PEELED AND DEVEINED, TAILS LEFT INTACT
300 G (10½ OZ) BLACK MUSSELS, BEARDS REMOVED
2 TABLESPOONS CHOPPED FRESH FLAT-LEAF (ITALIAN) PARSLEY
FRESHLY GROUND BLACK PEPPER

Heat 2 teaspoons of the oil in a large saucepan over medium-high heat. Add the chorizo and cook, stirring occasionally, for 6–7 minutes until it is crisp. Remove from the pan and set aside.

Reduce the heat to medium and add the remaining oil to the pan. Add the shallots and sprinkle with sea salt. Cook, stirring frequently, for 5 minutes, or until soft. Add the garlic, paprika and cayenne and cook, stirring, for another minute. Add the rice and stir to coat the grains with oil. Add the tomatoes, saffron, pepper and stock. Bring to the boil and then reduce the heat to low, cover and cook, stirring occasionally, for 15–20 minutes until the rice is almost tender.

Add the beans, prawns and mussels and return the chorizo to the pan. Cover and cook for another 10 minutes, or until the mussels have opened and the prawns are cooked through (discard any mussels that haven't opened after this time). Stir through the parsley and season to taste with salt and pepper.

PORTUGUESE CUSTARD TARTS

MAKES 12

3 EGG YOLKS
115 G (4 OZ/½ CUP) CASTER (SUPERFINE) SUGAR
2 TABLESPOONS CORNFLOUR (CORNSTARCH)
230 ML (7¾ FL OZ) CREAM
170 ML (5½ FL OZ/⅔ CUP) MILK
2 TEASPOONS NATURAL VANILLA EXTRACT
1 SHEET READY-ROLLED PUFF PASTRY

Put the egg yolks, sugar and cornflour in a saucepan and whisk together. Gradually whisk in the cream and milk until smooth. Place the pan over medium heat and cook, stirring, until the mixture thickens and comes to the boil. Remove from the heat and stir in the vanilla extract. Transfer the custard to a bowl, cover the surface with plastic wrap to prevent a skin forming and leave to cool.

Preheat the oven to 190°C (375°F/Gas 5). Lightly grease a 12-hole 80 ml (2½ fl oz/⅓ cup) muffin tin. Cut the pastry sheet in half, put one half on top of the other and set aside for 5 minutes. Roll up the pastry tightly from the short end and cut the pastry log into twelve 1 cm (½ inch) rounds. Lay each pastry round on a lightly floured surface and use a rolling pin to roll out until each is 10 cm (4 inches) in diameter.

Press the pastry rounds into the muffin tin. Spoon the cooled custard into the pastry cases and bake for 20–25 minutes, or until the pastry and custard are golden. Leave the tarts in the tin for 5 minutes, then transfer to a wire rack to cool completely.

PISCO SOUR

MAKES 2

125 ML (4 FL OZ/½ CUP) PISCO
3 TABLESPOONS LIME JUICE
1 TABLESPOON SUGAR SYRUP
1 EGG WHITE
ICE
ANGOSTURA BITTERS

Put the pisco, lime juice, sugar syrup and egg white into a shaker half-filled with ice and shake for 1 minute. Pour into chilled champagne flutes and garnish with a drop of bitters.

"This is my idea of perfect party food. The tarts are a less formal way to serve dessert."

DINNER DATE

MY SPAGHETTI MARINARA

SERVES 2

200 G (7 OZ) SPAGHETTI
2 TABLESPOONS OLIVE OIL
300 G (10½ OZ) RAW KING PRAWNS (SHRIMP), PEELED, DEVEINED AND CHOPPED
150 G (5½ OZ) SQUID, CLEANED AND CUT INTO THIN STRIPS
1 GARLIC CLOVE, CRUSHED
SMALL HANDFUL FRESH MINT LEAVES
SMALL HANDFUL FRESH BASIL LEAVES
LARGE HANDFUL FLAT-LEAF (ITALIAN) PARSLEY LEAVES
1 TABLESPOON SALTED BABY CAPERS, RINSED
2 ROMA (PLUM) TOMATOES, ROUGHLY CHOPPED
PINCH OF RED CHILLI FLAKES
SEA SALT
FRESHLY GROUND BLACK PEPPER

Cook the spaghetti in a large pan of lightly salted boiling water according to the packet instructions, or until al dente. Drain well.

Meanwhile, heat 1 tablespoon of the olive oil in a frying pan over medium heat. Add the prawns, squid and garlic and cook, stirring, for 1–2 minutes, or until the prawns are just cooked through and coated in the garlic. Remove from the heat and set aside.

Put the mint, basil, parsley, capers, tomatoes, chilli flakes and remaining oil in a blender and mix to a smooth paste (adding a little more olive oil if necessary). Season with salt and pepper.

Put the seafood and the herb dressing in a large bowl. Add the hot pasta and toss to coat in the sauce. Serve immediately.

MOLTEN CHOCOLATE PUDDINGS

SERVES 2

50 G (1¾ OZ) UNSALTED BUTTER, PLUS A LITTLE FOR GREASING
50 G (1¾ OZ) DARK CHOCOLATE, CHOPPED
1 EGG, PLUS 1 EXTRA EGG YOLK
1½ TABLESPOONS CASTER (SUPERFINE) SUGAR
1 TEASPOON PLAIN (ALL-PURPOSE) FLOUR

TO SERVE
UNSWEETENED COCOA POWDER, TO DUST
CREME FRAICHE

Preheat the oven to 220°C (425°F/Gas 7). Butter two 250 ml (9 fl oz/1 cup) ovenproof ramekins and dust with cocoa powder, shaking out any excess.

Melt the chocolate and butter together in a bowl over a pan of gently simmering water. While the chocolate is melting, with an electric whisk, beat the egg, egg yolk and sugar until pale and thick.

Pour the melted chocolate into the egg mixture. Sift in the flour and gently fold in. Spoon into the ramekins and bake for 10 minutes. Serve either in the ramekins or turned out onto serving plates. Dust with cocoa and serve with crème fraiche.

"This has become a modern classic for restaurant menus and it's one of the most romantic desserts I can think of. Great for sharing."

There's really no such thing as a typical Sunday in sunday our house, but my favourite Sundays are definitely lazy ones. My idea of heaven would be a stack of newspapers and no plans other than to read them. (In reality, the kids allow me about five minutes with the papers, but I can dream...)

The perfect Sunday would definitely be one with no plans. Imagine the luxury of waking up on Sunday morning with absolutely nothing to do. I can't wait until the girls are old enough to bring me breakfast in bed, but until that time comes we usually have a gang of friends over on Sunday morning. Brunch is another of those great Aussie traditions, and Sunday morning's a great time to get together with friends and family, especially when there are kids involved. If, like me, your days of partying late on a Saturday night are way behind you, then Sunday brunch can be a lot of fun. And, even if you've had a late night, Sunday's the one day of the week when it's perfectly acceptable (in my book, anyway) to eat breakfast halfway through the afternoon. We serve quite a lot of breakfasts at 3 pm on Sunday in the restaurants... I don't know what that says about the nocturnal habits of Sydneysiders.

The closest thing we have to a Sunday tradition in our family is dim sum in Chinatown. One of my earliest and happiest food memories is being taken to dim sum with a schoolfriend when I was seven. I can even remember what I ate — steamed sweet pork buns — which I thought were the best thing I'd ever tasted. Edie, Inès and Bunny seem to be taking after me in that respect; they love the energy and organized chaos of the dim sum experience — it's like theatre. Hundreds of people in one restaurant and, if the kids are screaming, nobody can hear them! Even after twelve years in the business, I still love the buzz of restaurants. I can't resist the sense of community and the energy that comes from a room full of people enjoying good food and conversation. As a kid I never wanted to go to amusement parks or anything, just restaurants. My idea of excitement was dinner at the local Chinese with my parents (although I seem to remember that falling asleep under the table was a favourite trick).

When I was growing up, the Sunday roast was an important tradition. Actually, because Dad was a butcher, it was a roast dinner every night of the week in our house. I have no idea how my Mum managed that! We usually save our roasts for Sundays now. As I get older I'm growing to love the cold and appreciate the beauty of winter — possibly because it means roast potatoes for lunch, making stock with the leftovers and then cooking up an enormous pot of soup for Sunday supper. I make vast quantities and freeze what's left for later in the week. There's nothing like a thermos flask of hot soup for a bit of soul-warming on a grey midweek lunchtime.

BIG BREAKFASTS

HOME FRIES

SERVES 4

4 LARGE FLOURY POTATOES (SUCH AS DESIREE), WASHED BUT NOT PEELED
1 TABLESPOON OLIVE OIL
1 TABLESPOON BUTTER, DICED
1 TEASPOON GROUND CUMIN
1 TEASPOON PAPRIKA
SEA SALT
FRESHLY GROUND BLACK PEPER
1 RED ONION, ROUGHLY CHOPPED
1 GREEN PEPPER (CAPSICUM), ROUGHLY CHOPPED
2 TABLESPOONS CHOPPED FRESH CORIANDER (CILANTRO)
GREEN TABASCO

TO SERVE
FRIED EGGS

Preheat the oven to 200°C (400°F/Gas 6). Put the whole potatoes in a steamer and steam for 20 minutes, or until almost tender, leaving them slightly underdone. Set aside until cool enough to handle, then cut them into bite-sized chunks and put in a large roasting tin. Drizzle with the olive oil and toss to coat. Dot with the butter, sprinkle with cumin and paprika, season with salt and pepper and roast in the oven for 20 minutes.

Turn the potatoes and add the onion and pepper to the tin. Roast for a further 15 minutes, or until crispy and golden. Toss with the coriander and a few drops of Tabasco. Serve topped with fried eggs.

"I'm a huge fan of savoury breakfasts, and I always try to use organic eggs. Green Tabasco sauce is my new obsession — I love its tangy sourness."

BAKED BEANS

SERVES 6

1 TABLESPOON OLIVE OIL
1 ONION, FINELY CHOPPED
100 G (3½ OZ) PANCETTA, CHOPPED
1 GARLIC CLOVE, CRUSHED
2 ANCHOVIES, CHOPPED
1 TEASPOON FINELY CHOPPED FRESH THYME LEAVES
½ TEASPOON DRIED OREGANO
400 G (14 OZ) TIN CHOPPED TOMATOES
2 X 400 G (14 OZ) TINS CANNELLINI BEANS, RINSED
SEA SALT
FRESHLY GROUND BLACK PEPPER

Preheat the oven to 160°C (315°F/Gas 2–3). Heat the olive oil in a large flameproof casserole over medium heat. Add the onion and cook, stirring, for 5–6 minutes until the onion is soft. Add the pancetta and cook, stirring occasionally, for 5 minutes, or until slightly crisp. Add the garlic, anchovies, thyme and oregano and cook, stirring, for another minute.

Add the tomatoes and 125 ml (4 fl oz/½ cup) of water, bring to the boil and then reduce the heat to simmer for 10 minutes. Stir in the beans, put a lid on the casserole and bake in the oven for 30 minutes. Season with salt and pepper.

CHICKEN SAUSAGES WITH SPICY TOMATO RELISH

SERVES 6

3 VINE-RIPENED TOMATOES, QUARTERED, SEEDED AND FINELY SLICED
2 LARGE RED CHILLIES, SEEDED AND FINELY SLICED
2 SPRING ONIONS (SCALLIONS), SLICED
SMALL HANDFUL FRESH FLAT-LEAF (ITALIAN) PARSLEY LEAVES
1 TEASPOON LEMON JUICE
1 TABLESPOON EXTRA VIRGIN OLIVE OIL
SEA SALT
FRESHLY GROUND BLACK PEPPER
1 TABLESPOON OLIVE OIL
12 CHICKEN SAUSAGES

To make the relish, mix together the tomatoes, chilli, spring onions, parsley, lemon juice, extra virgin olive oil, salt and pepper and set aside.

Heat the olive oil in a large frying pan over medium-high heat. Cook the sausages for 6–8 minutes on each side, or until golden brown. Slice each sausage in half and cook, cut-side-down, for another couple of minutes until golden. Serve with the spicy tomato relish.

"Slicing the sausages in half and cooking for a couple of minutes gives them a great texture (and you don't feel so greedy having seconds when it's only half a sausage)."

SUNDAY ROASTS

TURKEY WITH ALL THE TRIMMINGS

ROLLED TURKEY BREAST WITH PISTACHIO AND CRANBERRY STUFFING

SERVES 4–6

1–1.5 KG (ABOUT 3 LB) BONELESS TURKEY BREAST, WITH SKIN
PISTACHIO AND CRANBERRY STUFFING, COOLED, BELOW
1 TABLESPOON MELTED BUTTER

Preheat the oven to 190°C (375°F/Gas 5). Put the turkey breast, skin-side-down, on a board. Spoon the cooled stuffing down the middle of the breast and then roll up the turkey to enclose the stuffing. Tie the turkey with kitchen string every 2 cm (about an inch) to secure and then place in a large roasting tin. Brush the entire surface of the turkey with melted butter.

Roast for 40 minutes, or until golden brown and the juices run clear when you poke a skewer into the thickest part of the turkey. Cover loosely with foil and leave to rest for 15 minutes before carving. Serve with cranberry relish, overleaf.

PISTACHIO AND CRANBERRY STUFFING

40 G (1½ OZ) BUTTER
1 ONION, CHOPPED
100 G (3½ OZ) PANCETTA, RIND REMOVED, CHOPPED
1 GARLIC CLOVE, CRUSHED
120 G (4 OZ/1½ CUPS) FRESH WHITE BREADCRUMBS
1 TABLESPOON CHOPPED FRESH SAGE
100 G (3½ OZ/⅔ CUP) CRAISINS (SWEETENED DRIED CRANBERRIES)
50 G (1¾ OZ/⅓ CUP) PISTACHIO NUTS, ROUGHLY CHOPPED
SEA SALT
FRESHLY GROUND BLACK PEPPER

Heat the butter in a large frying pan over medium heat. Add the onion and cook, stirring occasionally, for 3–4 minutes until softened. Add the pancetta and cook, stirring occasionally, for 5 minutes until cooked through. Add the garlic and cook for another minute. Tip everything into a large bowl. Add the breadcrumbs, sage, craisins and pistachios, season well and stir together. Leave to cool completely before using.

CRANBERRY RELISH

SERVES 10

175 G (6 OZ) CRAISINS (SWEETENED DRIED CRANBERRIES)
3 TABLESPOONS CASTER (SUPERFINE) SUGAR
FINELY GRATED ZEST AND JUICE OF 1 ORANGE

Put the craisins, sugar, orange zest and juice in a saucepan over medium heat with 250 ml (9 fl oz/ 1 cup) of water and cook, stirring occasionally, for 12 minutes, or until the craisins are softened and the sauce is slightly reduced and syrupy. Serve warm or at room temperature with roast turkey.

ROAST PUMPKIN AND RED ONION WITH HONEY DRESSING

SERVES 4

2 RED ONIONS, UNPEELED AND QUARTERED
800 G (1 LB 12 OZ) PUMPKIN (SQUASH), UNPEELED AND CUT INTO WEDGES
1/2 TEASPOON RED CHILLI FLAKES
3 TABLESPOONS EXTRA VIRGIN OLIVE OIL
SEA SALT
80 ML (2 1/2 FL OZ) HONEY
80 ML (2 1/2 FL OZ/1/3 CUP) RED WINE VINEGAR
LARGE HANDFUL FRESH MINT LEAVES

Preheat the oven to 200°C (400°F/Gas 6). Put the onion, pumpkin, red chilli flakes, olive oil and salt in a large baking dish and toss well to coat the vegetables with oil. Roast for 40–45 minutes until the pumpkin is soft and golden.

Put the honey and red wine vinegar in a small saucepan, bring to the boil and then simmer for 5 minutes. Put the pumpkin and onion in a serving dish, drizzle with the honey dressing and sprinkle with mint leaves.

GREEN BEANS AND WATERCRESS

SERVES 4–6

200 G (7 OZ) GREEN BEANS, TOPPED
1 BUNCH WATERCRESS
2 TABLESPOONS EXTRA VIRGIN OLIVE OIL
1 TABLESPOON LEMON JUICE
SEA SALT
FRESHLY GROUND BLACK PEPPER

Blanch the beans in a saucepan of boiling water until bright green and crisply tender. Rinse under cold running water and drain well.

Pick the leaves from the watercress and place in a bowl with the beans. Whisk together the olive oil and lemon juice, season with salt and pepper and toss with the salad. Serve immediately.

APPLE AND CHERRY TARTS

MAKES 8

375 G (13 OZ/3 CUPS) PLAIN (ALL-PURPOSE) FLOUR
90 G (3¼ OZ/¾ CUP) ICING (CONFECTIONERS') SUGAR, SIFTED
PINCH OF SALT
250 G (9 OZ) UNSALTED BUTTER, CHILLED AND CUBED
90 ML (3 FL OZ) ICED WATER
450 G (1 LB) PITTED CHERRIES (FROZEN ARE FINE)
3 GRANNY SMITH APPLES, PEELED, CORED AND CUT INTO 2 CM (¾ INCH) CUBES
1½ TABLESPOONS CORNFLOUR (CORNSTARCH)
4 TABLESPOONS CASTER (SUPERFINE) SUGAR
1 EGG WHITE, LIGHTLY BEATEN

To make the pastry, whiz the flour, icing sugar and salt in a food processor until combined. Add the butter and process until the mixture resembles coarse breadcrumbs. Add the iced water and process until the dough comes together in a ball. Wrap in plastic wrap and chill for 30 minutes.

Preheat the oven to 180°C (350°F/Gas 4). Lightly grease eight 125 ml (4 fl oz/½ cup) muffin holes and line with strips of baking paper hanging over the edges (these will help you lift out the tarts). Roll out the pastry on a lightly floured work surface until it is 3 mm (⅛ inch) thick and then use it to line the muffin holes. Cut out eight pastry circles to fit the tops.

Mix together the cherries, apple, cornflour and sugar and spoon into the pastry cases. Top with the pastry circles and crimp the edges together with a fork. Brush the pastry with egg white. Bake for 35–40 minutes, or until golden.

"These little tarts are inspired by the mince pies that I love serving at Christmas."

SUNDAY ROAST BEEF

STANDING RIB ROAST

SERVES 4–6

2 KG (4 LB 8 OZ) STANDING RIB BEEF ROAST
1 TABLESPOON OLIVE OIL
SEA SALT
FRESHLY GROUND BLACK PEPPER
3 RED ONIONS, QUARTERED

Preheat the oven to 200°C (400°F/Gas 6). Rub the beef with olive oil and season with salt and pepper. Heat a large frying pan over high heat. Add the beef and cook for 1–2 minutes on each side, or until browned all over. Transfer the beef to a large roasting tin.

Roast the beef for 30 minutes and then add the onions to the tin. Roast for another 40–50 minutes for medium cooked meat. Remove, cover loosely with foil and leave to rest for at least 15 minutes.

POTATO AND CELERIAC GRATIN

SERVES 6

2 TABLESPOONS OLIVE OIL
2 ONIONS, THINLY SLICED
2 GARLIC CLOVES, CRUSHED
750 G (1 LB 10 OZ) CELERIAC, PEELED, HALVED AND VERY THINLY SLICED
500 G (1 LB 2 OZ) POTATOES (SUCH AS DESIREE), PEELED AND VERY THINLY SLICED
SEA SALT
FRESHLY GROUND BLACK PEPPER
1 TABLESPOON FRESH THYME LEAVES
500 ML (17 FL OZ/2 CUPS) CHICKEN STOCK

Preheat the oven to 180°C (350°F/Gas 4). Heat the olive oil in a large frying pan over medium heat. Add the onion and cook, stirring occasionally, for 6–7 minutes until soft and light golden. Add the garlic and cook, stirring, for another minute. Remove from the heat.

Lightly grease a 1.5 litre (52 fl oz/6 cup) gratin dish. Place a layer of celeriac in the base of the dish, followed by a layer of potato, seasoning between the layers. Sprinkle some of the onion and thyme leaves over this. Continue the layers, finishing with potato and some thyme. Pour the stock over the top and press down on the potatoes to cover everything with stock. Cover with foil and bake for 35 minutes. Remove the foil and bake for a further 20 minutes, or until the vegetables are tender and golden. Leave for 5 minutes before serving.

BUTTER LETTUCE, CUCUMBER AND RADISH SALAD

SERVES 4

1 FULL HEAD BUTTER LETTUCE, SHREDDED
1 SMALL LEBANESE (SHORT) CUCUMBER, THINLY SLICED
3 RADISHES, THINLY SLICED
1 SMALL LEMON, PEEL AND PITH REMOVED, DIVIDED INTO SEGMENTS
1 TABLESPOON OLIVE OIL
SEA SALT
FRESHLY GROUND BLACK PEPPER

Put the butter lettuce, cucumber, radish and lemon segments in a salad bowl and drizzle with olive oil. Season with salt and pepper.

"No matter what time of year, or how cold and wintry it is, I always love a fresh salad. This one's a favourite."

STICKY DATE CAKE WITH BUTTERSCOTCH SAUCE

SERVES 10

300 G (10½ OZ) PITTED DATES, CHOPPED
1 TEASPOON BICARBONATE OF SODA (BAKING SODA)
70 G (2½ OZ) UNSALTED BUTTER, DICED
170 G (6 OZ/¾ CUP) CASTER (SUPERFINE) SUGAR
1 TEASPOON NATURAL VANILLA EXTRACT
2 EGGS, LIGHTLY BEATEN
185 G (6½ OZ/1½ CUPS) SELF-RAISING FLOUR, SIFTED

TO SERVE
BUTTERSCOTCH SAUCE, BELOW
VANILLA ICE CREAM

Preheat the oven to 180°C (350°F/Gas 4). Grease and line the base of a 20 cm (8 inch) round cake tin with baking paper.

Put the dates in a pan with 250 ml (9 fl oz/1 cup) water. Cook, stirring occasionally, for 5–6 minutes until the dates are soft and the water has been absorbed. Remove from the heat and stir in the bicarbonate of soda and butter. Set aside for 10 minutes to cool slightly.

Transfer to a large mixing bowl, add the sugar, vanilla and eggs and stir well. Fold in the sifted flour until combined. Spoon into the tin and bake for 50 minutes, or until a skewer poked into the middle comes out clean. Leave in the tin for 5 minutes, then turn out and cool on a wire rack. Serve with warm butterscotch sauce and ice cream.

BUTTERSCOTCH SAUCE

MAKES 500 ML (17 FL OZ/2 CUPS)

185 G (6½ OZ/1 CUP) SOFT BROWN SUGAR
200 ML (7 FL OZ) CREAM
150 G (5½ OZ) UNSALTED BUTTER

Heat the sugar, cream and butter in a saucepan over medium heat, stirring to dissolve the sugar. Bring to a simmer and cook over low heat for 3 minutes. Pour over the sticky date cake to serve.

SUNDAY LUNCH, GREEK-STYLE

SLOW-COOKED GREEK LAMB

SERVES 6

2 KG (4 LB 8 OZ) LEG OF LAMB ON THE BONE, TRIMMED
SEA SALT
FRESHLY GROUND BLACK PEPPER
SMALL HANDFUL FRESH OREGANO LEAVES
JUICE OF 1 LEMON, PLUS 1 LEMON, QUARTERED
3 TABLESPOONS WHITE WINE
2 TABLESPOONS OLIVE OIL
4 LARGE POTATOES (SUCH AS DESIREE), PEELED AND CUT INTO CHUNKS
175 G (6 OZ/1 CUP) LARGE GREEN OLIVES

Preheat the oven to 220°C (425°F/Gas 7). Put the lamb in a large roasting tin and season well with salt and pepper. Sprinkle with the oregano and pour over the lemon juice and wine. Drizzle with the olive oil and roast for 20 minutes, or until the lamb is browned.

Add 125 ml (4 fl oz/½ cup) of water to the roasting tin and cover the tin with foil. Reduce the oven to 160°C (315°F/Gas 2–3) and roast the lamb for another 1½ hours. Arrange the potato and lemon quarters around the lamb and return to the oven for another 2 hours, turning the potatoes at least once during this time and basting the lamb with the pan juices. The lamb should be very tender.

Remove the lamb from the tin and set aside to rest before slicing. Increase the oven to 220°C (425°F/Gas 7). Add the olives to the tin with the potatoes and return to the oven for 20 minutes, or until the potatoes are golden. Serve with the lamb, with some pan juices spooned over the top.

STEWED BEANS IN TOMATO

SERVES 6

1 TABLESPOON OLIVE OIL
1 ONION, CHOPPED
2 GARLIC CLOVES, THINLY SLICED
400 G (14 OZ) TIN CHOPPED TOMATOES
800 G (1 LB 12 OZ) GREEN BEANS, TOPPED
SEA SALT
FRESHLY GROUND BLACK PEPPER

Preheat the oven to 160°C (315°F/Gas 2–3). Heat the oil in a large flameproof casserole over medium heat. Cook the onion, stirring, for 5 minutes, then add the garlic and cook for another minute. Add the tomatoes and 250 ml (9 fl oz/1 cup) of water and bring to the boil. Add the beans. Transfer to the oven and bake for 1 hour. Season before serving.

CUCUMBER AND YOGHURT RELISH

SERVES 6

250 ML (9 FL OZ/1 CUP) THICK GREEK YOGHURT
1 LEBANESE (SHORT) CUCUMBER, SEEDED AND FINELY DICED
2 TABLESPOONS CHOPPED FRESH FLAT-LEAF (ITALIAN) PARSLEY
1 TABLESPOON LEMON JUICE
SEA SALT
FRESHLY GROUND BLACK PEPPER

Stir together the yoghurt, cucumber, parsley and lemon juice and season with salt and pepper.

SEMOLINA SYRUP CAKE

SERVES 12–16

125 G (4½ OZ) UNSALTED BUTTER, SOFTENED
220 G (7¾ OZ/1 CUP) CASTER (SUPERFINE) SUGAR
250 ML (9 FL OZ/1 CUP) THICK GREEK YOGHURT
3 EGGS, SEPARATED
1 TEASPOON FINELY GRATED ORANGE ZEST
125 G (4½ OZ/1 CUP) PLAIN (ALL-PURPOSE) FLOUR
125 G (4½ OZ/1 CUP) FINE SEMOLINA
2 TEASPOONS BAKING POWDER
55 G (2 OZ/½ CUP) GROUND ALMONDS
80 ML (2½ FL OZ/⅓ CUP) MILK
BLANCHED ALMONDS, TO DECORATE

ORANGE BLOSSOM SYRUP
220 G (7¾ OZ/1 CUP) CASTER (SUPERFINE) SUGAR
1 TEASPOON ORANGE BLOSSOM WATER

Preheat your oven to 180°C (350°F/Gas 4). Grease and line a 22 cm (8½ inch) square cake tin with baking paper, letting the paper hang over the side of the tin to help you lift out the cake later.

Cream the butter and sugar together with electric beaters. Beat in the yoghurt, egg yolks and orange zest. Sift in the flour, semolina and baking powder and mix to combine. Mix in the almonds and milk. In another bowl, beat the egg whites until soft peaks form, then carefully fold into the batter.

Pour into the tin, decorate the top of the cake with blanched almonds and bake for 40 minutes, or until the cake is golden and a skewer poked into the middle comes out clean. Leave to cool in the tin.

To make the syrup, put the sugar, orange blossom water and 250 ml (9 fl oz/1 cup) of water in a small saucepan. Cook, stirring to dissolve the sugar, then bring to the boil and simmer for 5 minutes. Pour the hot syrup over the cake in the tin and leave it to cool completely.

SOUP SUPPERS

LIGHT LAKSA

SERVES 4

1 TEASPOON PEANUT OIL
1 TABLESPOON RED CURRY PASTE
1 LITRE (35 FL OZ/4 CUPS) CHICKEN STOCK
150 ML (5 FL OZ) COCONUT MILK
2 MAKRUT (KAFFIR LIME) LEAVES, PLUS THINLY SLICED LEAVES TO GARNISH
3 CM (ABOUT 1 INCH) PIECE OF FRESH GINGER, PEELED AND SLICED
500 G (1 LB 2 OZ) BONELESS CHICKEN BREASTS
SOFT BROWN SUGAR AND LIME JUICE, TO TASTE
150 G (5½ OZ) RICE VERMICELLI, SOAKED IN HOT WATER AND DRAINED
1 BUNCH BABY BOK CHOY (PAK CHOY)
90 G (3¼ OZ/1 CUP) TRIMMED BEAN SPROUTS

Heat the peanut oil in a large saucepan over medium heat. Add the curry paste and cook, stirring, for 1–2 minutes, or until fragrant. Add the stock, coconut milk, makrut leaves and ginger.

Increase the heat to high and bring to the boil. Then reduce the heat to very low, add the chicken, cover the pan and poach the chicken gently for 7 minutes, or until just cooked through. Remove the chicken and set aside to cool slightly, then shred.

Season the soup with the brown sugar and lime juice, to taste. Divide the rice vermicelli, shredded chicken, bok choy and bean sprouts among four large bowls. Pour in the hot soup and garnish with thinly sliced makrut leaves.

"Laksa can be really rich but, by using stock and just a little bit of coconut milk, you get the great flavour without the heaviness."

WHITE BEAN AND CHORIZO SOUP

SERVES 6

1 TEASPOON OLIVE OIL
1 CHORIZO SAUSAGE (ABOUT 150 G/5½ OZ), DICED
1 LARGE ONION, THINLY SLICED
2 CELERY STALKS, DICED
2 GARLIC CLOVES, CRUSHED
2 TEASPOONS CHOPPED FRESH THYME
1 TEASPOON PAPRIKA
2 TOMATOES, DICED
1 LITRE (35 FL OZ/4 CUPS) CHICKEN STOCK
2 X 400 G (14 OZ) TINS CANNELLINI BEANS, RINSED
SEA SALT
FRESHLY GROUND BLACK PEPPER

Heat the olive oil in a large pan over high heat and cook the chorizo for 3–4 minutes until crisp. Drain on kitchen paper.

Reduce the heat to medium-low, add the onion and celery to the pan and cook, stirring occasionally, for 6–7 minutes until softened. Add the garlic, thyme and paprika and cook, stirring, for 1–2 minutes until fragrant. Add the tomatoes and cook for another minute.

Return the chorizo to the pan with the stock and bring to the boil, then reduce the heat and simmer, stirring occasionally, for 10 minutes. Add the beans and cook for another 5 minutes. Season with salt and pepper before serving.

"Heaven? That would be Sunday night at home, with the girls bathed and in bed, a glass of wine, and a pot of soup on the stove."

"Soup is that almost strange combination of health and comfort food. It's hard to resist."

SWEETCORN CHOWDER

SERVES 4–6

1 TABLESPOON OLIVE OIL
2 BACON RASHERS, CHOPPED
1 ONION, ROUGHLY CHOPPED
SEA SALT
FRESHLY GROUND BLACK PEPPER
1.5 LITRES (52 FL OZ/6 CUPS) CHICKEN STOCK
500 G (1 LB 2 OZ) POTATOES, PEELED AND DICED
600 G (1 LB 5 OZ/3 CUPS) CORN KERNELS, CUT FROM THE COB

TO SERVE
CORIANDER (CILANTRO) LEAVES
2 TABLESPOONS THINLY SLICED SPRING ONIONS (SCALLIONS)

Heat the olive oil in a large saucepan over medium-high heat, add the bacon and cook for about 5 minutes until crisp. Remove the bacon from the pan.

Add the onion, salt and pepper to the pan and cook for 6–7 minutes, stirring occasionally. Add the stock and potatoes and bring to the boil. Cook for 5 minutes, then add the corn and cook for another 5 minutes, until the potatoes and corn are tender.

Purée half the soup and return to the pan. Bring back to the boil before serving, scattered with bacon, coriander and spring onion.

"This was the first thing I ever cooked, at the age of seven. It's remained a constant in my life. It feels like an old friend."

TOMATO AND LENTIL SOUP

SERVES 4–6

2 KG (4 LB 8 OZ) VINE-RIPENED TOMATOES, HALVED
6 GARLIC CLOVES, PEELED
1 SMALL CARROT, DICED
3 TABLESPOONS EXTRA VIRGIN OLIVE OIL
2 TABLESPOONS SEA SALT
FRESHLY GROUND BLACK PEPPER
90 G (3¼ OZ/⅓ CUP) RED LENTILS
300 ML (10½ FL OZ) CHICKEN OR VEGETABLE STOCK

TO SERVE
FRESH BASIL LEAVES
EXTRA VIRGIN OLIVE OIL

Preheat the oven to 200°C (400°F/Gas 6). Put the tomatoes, garlic and carrot in a roasting tin. Drizzle with olive oil and sprinkle with salt and pepper. Cover with foil and bake for 1½ hours. Uncover and bake for another 30 minutes, or until the vegetables are well cooked.

Transfer the vegetables to a food processor and blend to a smoothish mixture with some texture. (If you prefer a completely smooth soup, you can pass it through a sieve, but I prefer it with a bit more texture.)

Pour the soup back into the pan and bring to the boil over high heat. Add the lentils and stock, return to the boil and then reduce the heat to low and simmer, stirring frequently, for 15–20 minutes until the lentils are tender. Serve in soup bowls, topped with basil leaves and a drizzle of extra virgin olive oil.

STOCKS

CHICKEN STOCK

MAKES 2–3 LITRES (ABOUT 90 FL OZ/10 CUPS)

1 ORGANIC CHICKEN, RINSED AND PATTED DRY (OR USE 1.5 KG/3 LB 5 OZ CHICKEN BONES)
2 ONIONS, QUARTERED
2 CARROTS, PEELED AND ROUGHLY CHOPPED
2 LEAFY CELERY STALKS, ROUGHLY CHOPPED
1 TEASPOON BLACK PEPPERCORNS
1 BAY LEAF
HANDFUL OF FRESH FLAT-LEAF (ITALIAN) PARSLEY

Put all the ingredients and 4 litres (140 fl oz/16 cups) of cold water in a large stockpot and slowly bring to the boil. Reduce the heat to very low and simmer gently for 2–3 hours. Skim off any scum or excess fat that comes to the top of the stock. Strain and leave to cool before refrigerating or freezing. If you used the whole chicken, shred the meat and use for poached chicken sandwiches or soup.

VEGETABLE STOCK

MAKES ABOUT 2 LITRES (70 FL OZ/8 CUPS)

2 TABLESPOONS OLIVE OIL
500 G (1 LB 2 OZ) ONIONS, ROUGHLY CHOPPED
500 G (1 LB 2 OZ) CARROTS, ROUGHLY CHOPPED
250 G (8 OZ) PARSNIPS, PEELED AND ROUGHLY CHOPPED
2 LEAFY CELERY STALKS, ROUGHLY CHOPPED
6 GARLIC CLOVES, CRUSHED
2 LEEKS, WHITE PART ONLY, ROUGHLY CHOPPED
4 SPRING ONIONS (SCALLIONS), ROUGHLY CHOPPED
HANDFUL OF FRESH FLAT-LEAF (ITALIAN) PARSLEY
1 TEASPOON BLACK PEPPERCORNS
4 BAY LEAVES
1 TABLESPOON SEA SALT

Heat the oil in a stockpot over medium heat. Add the onion, carrot, parsnip, celery and garlic and fry gently for 5 minutes. Add the remaining ingredients and 2 litres (70 fl oz/8 cups) of water and bring to the boil. Reduce the heat and simmer for 1 hour. Strain and leave to cool before refrigerating or freezing.

INDEX

A

apples
  apple and cherry tarts 227
  apple, dried cherry and almond loaf 10
  stewed apple with blueberries and yoghurt 46
apricot and cinnamon cake 193
artichoke salad, rice and broad bean 167
asparagus risotto, oven-baked chicken and 128

B

baked beans 220
bananas
  banana sour cream hotcakes with date and pecan butter 182
  banana, strawberry and orange smoothie 82
  vanilla rice porridge with caramelized bananas 42
beans
  baked beans 220
  beans stewed in tomato 236
  chilli bean burritos with corn salsa 56
  corn with French beans 203
  egg noodles with tofu and green beans 122
  green beans and watercress 227
  lentil, bean and parsley salad 20
  pink grapefruit, bean and cashew salad with lime dressing 169
  rice, broad bean and artichoke salad 167
  steak with cherry tomatoes and cannellini beans 66
  white bean and chorizo soup 242
  white bean, tuna and lemon salad 51
beef
  beef and noodle stir-fry with Asian greens 109
  standing rib roast 230
  steak with cherry tomatoes and cannellini beans 66
berry hotcakes 13
berry yoghurt muffins 120
blinis, sweetcorn 162
blt 154
bread, rosemary and olive spelt 173
breakfasts
  apple, dried cherry and almond loaf 10
  banana sour cream hotcakes with date and pecan butter 182
  berry hotcakes 13
  breakfast blt 154
  croque madame 152
  French raisin toast with cinnamon 80
  home fries 218
  mix-and-go muesli 42
  real muesli bars 118
  vanilla rice porridge with caramelized bananas 42
broccolini and tofu sambal 33
burger 86
burritos, chilli bean with corn salsa 56
butter lettuce, cucumber and radish salad 232
butterscotch sauce 233

C

cabbage, sweet and sour 69
cakes
  chocolate hazelnut ricotta cake with cinnamon poached figs 138
  fresh apricot and cinnamon 193
  lamingtons 192
  lemon pound cake 188
  semolina syrup cake 237
  sticky date cake with butterscotch sauce 233
caramel milkshake, real 90
caramel salmon 144
caramel sauce 90
casserole, chicken, tomato and fennel 132
cheat's pizza 49
chicken
  chicken and asparagus risotto, oven-baked 128
  chicken sausages with spicy tomato relish 222
  chicken, tomato and fennel casserole 132
  crispy chicken fingers 50
  fragrant chicken and spinach curry 141
  lemon chicken 196
  lime, paprika and honey glazed chicken 73
  oven-baked chicken and asparagus risotto 128
  ricotta- and herb-stuffed roast chicken 202
  sandwich 46
  spicy chicken meatballs 110
  spicy chicken thighs with cucumber and cashew salad 28
  stir-fried, with peanuts and cucumber 100
chicken stock 248
chickpea, burghul and parsley salad with marinated lamb 24
chilli
  broccolini and tofu sambal 33
  chilli bean burritos with corn salsa 56
  chilli and garlic prawns with asparagus 198
  crisp-skin salmon with sweet chilli dressing 106
Chinese rice, baked, with peas and ginger 198
chocolate
  chocolate hazelnut ricotta cake with cinnamon poached figs 138
  hot chocolate 90

molten chocolate puddings 212
peanut butter and chocolate
    chunk cookies 92
chorizo, potato and red pepper
    frittata 184
chowder, sweetcorn 246
cinnamon poached figs 138
cocktail sauce 187
coconut custard 199
coconut dressing 18
cookies
    iced jumbles 93
    oatmeal and raisin 45
    peanut butter and chocolate
        chunk 92
coriander pesto 62
coriander-crumbed lamb cutlets 158
corn
    corn with French beans 203
    corn and prawn fritters 156
    corn salsa 57
    sweetcorn blinis 162
    sweetcorn chowder 246
cranberry and pistachio stuffing 224
cranberry relish 226
crisp-skin salmon with sweet chilli
    dressing 106
crispy chicken fingers 50
croque madame 152
crudités, get-some-greens-in 92
cucumber
    cucumber and cashew salad 28
    cucumber and snow pea salad 147
    cucumber and yoghurt relish 237
    cumin, mint and coriander
        yoghurt 140
curry
    fragrant chicken and spinach 141
    lamb biryani 140
custard tarts, Portuguese 207

D
date and pecan butter 182
desserts
    baked nectarine crumbles 112
    chocolate hazelnut ricotta cake
        with cinnamon poached figs 138

fresh fruit plate with lemon grass
    syrup 147
golden syrup puddings 112
little steamed ginger puddings
    with coconut custard 199
molten chocolate puddings 212
pavlova with yoghurt cream and
    strawberries 176
poached nectarines with sweet
    vanilla ricotta 36
raisins in liqueur with ice cream
    and biscotti 74
raspberry, pistachio and rosewater
    semifreddo 203
roasted plums with almonds and
    cinnamon ice cream 74
dressings
    coconut 18
    lime 169
    shallot vinaigrette 187

F
fig smoothie, raspberry and 82
figs, cinnamon poached 138
fish
    caramel salmon 144
    fragrant fish parcels 168
    Moroccan fish stew 60
    pan-fried, with lime and chilli
        slaw 26
    salmon tartine 87
    salmon with mint and roast
        potato salad 70
    salmon with sweet chilli dressing
        106
    spaghettini with fish, chilli and
        parsley 54
    tuna daube 102
    whiting with tomato and sumac
        salad 96
see also seafood
French raisin toast 80
fries
    home fries 218
    sweet potato fries 87
frittata 184
fritters, zucchini 161

G
garlic toasts 133
ginger puddings 199
golden syrup puddings 112
grapefruit, bean and cashew salad,
    pink 169
gravlax and cream cheese topping
    13
green beans and watercress 227

H
haloumi open sandwich 84
hand-held prawns 156
herbed yoghurt 158
home fries 218
hotcakes
    banana sour cream, with date and
        pecan butter 182
    berry 13

I
iced jumbles 93
icing 93
icing, lemon butter 188

L
L.A. burger 86
laksa, light 241
lamb
    chickpea, burghul and parsley
        salad with marinated lamb 24
    coriander-crumbed cutlets 158
    lamb biryani 140
    slow-cooked Greek lamb 236
lamingtons 192
lemon
    lemon butter icing 188
    lemon chicken 196
    lemon pound cake 188
lentils
    lentil, bean and parsley salad 20
    tomato and lentil soup 247
lime
    lime and chilli slaw 26
    lime dressing 169
    lime, paprika and honey glazed
        chicken 73

M

mash, parmesan 105

miso, soba noodle and silken tofu broth 34

mix-and-go muesli 42

molten chocolate puddings 212

Moroccan fish stew 60

muesli, mix-and-go 42

muesli bars, real 118

muffins, berry yoghurt 120

mushroom and prosciutto pasta 130

N

nectarines

baked nectarine crumbles 112

poached, with sweet vanilla ricotta 36

noodles

egg noodles with tofu and green beans 122

miso, soba noodle and silken tofu broth 34

O

oatmeal and raisin cookies 45

orange blossom syrup 237

P

paella 206

parmesan mash 105

parsley pesto 63

pasta

baked tomato and mozzarella 127

creamy mushroom and prosciutto 130

my spaghetti marinara 210

spaghetti with garlic and spinach 98

spaghettini with fish, chilli and parsley 54

pavlova with yoghurt cream and strawberries 176

pea, feta and mint salad 16

peach and raspberry slice 51

peanuts

peanut butter and chocolate chunk cookies 92

stir-fried chicken with peanuts and cucumber 100

pepitas, spiced 162

pesto

coriander 62

parsley 63

walnut 62

pineapple, honeydew and mint smoothie 82

pink grapefruit, bean and cashew salad with lime dressing 169

pisco sour 207

pistachio and cranberry stuffing 224

pizza, cheat's 49

plums, roasted 74

pomegranate juice with prosecco 163

pork

L.A. burger 86

pork cutlets with apple sauce and sweet and sour cabbage 69

sausages with caramelized onions and parmesan mash 105

stir-fried, with hoisin and greens 124

porridge, vanilla rice, with caramelized bananas 42

Portuguese custard tarts 207

potatoes

chorizo, potato and red pepper frittata 184

mash, parmesan 105

potato and celeriac gratin 230

salmon with mint and roast potato salad 70

prawns

chilli and garlic prawns with asparagus 198

corn and prawn fritters 156

hand-held prawns 156

prawn salad with coconut dressing 18

puddings

golden syrup puddings 112

little steamed ginger puddings with coconut custard 199

molten chocolate puddings 212

pumpkin and red onion with honey dressing, roast 226

Q

quail, barbecued, with spiced salt and lemon 167

R

radicchio slaw 172

raisins in liqueur with ice cream and biscotti 74

raspberries

peach and raspberry slice 51

raspberry and fig smoothie 82

raspberry, pistachio and rosewater semifreddo 203

raspberry tarts 190

rice

baked Chinese rice with peas and ginger 198

oven-baked chicken and asparagus risotto 128

rice, broad bean and artichoke salad 167

ricotta- and herb-stuffed roast chicken 202

rosemary and olive spelt bread 173

S

salads

butter lettuce, cucumber and radish salad 232

chickpea, burghul and parsley salad with marinated lamb 24

cucumber and cashew 28

cucumber and snow pea 147

green beans and watercress 227

lentil, bean and parsley 20

lime and chilli slaw 26

pea, feta and mint 16

pink grapefruit, bean and cashew salad with lime dressing 169

prawn salad with coconut dressing 18

radicchio slaw 172

rice, broad bean and artichoke 167

spicy squid, with cucumber and
    capers 14
tomato and sumac 96
watercress, apple and witlof 133
white bean, tuna and lemon 51
salmon
    caramel salmon 144
    crisp-skin, with sweet chilli
        dressing 106
    salmon tartine 87
    salmon with mint and roast
        potato salad 70
salsa, corn 57
sambal, broccolini and tofu 33
sandwich, haloumi open 84
sandwich, my favourite 46
sauces
    butterscotch 233
    caramel 90
    cocktail 187
sausages
    with caramelized onions and
        parmesan mash 105
    chicken sausages with spicy
        tomato relish 222
    chorizo, potato and red pepper
        frittata 184
    with stewed peppers 172
    white bean and chorizo soup 242
seafood
    half-shell scallops with garlic and
        parsley breadcrumbs 161
    my spaghetti marinara 210
    paella 206
    shellfish plate 187
    spicy squid salad with cucumber
        and capers 14
see also fish; prawns
semifreddo 203
semolina syrup cake 237
shallot vinaigrette 187
shellfish plate 187
smoothies 82
soup
    light laksa 241
    miso, soba noodle and silken tofu
        broth 34

sweetcorn chowder 246
tomato and lentil 247
vegetable 23
white bean and chorizo 242
spaghetti marinara 210
spaghetti with garlic and spinach 98
spaghettini with fish, chilli and
    parsley 54
spelt bread 173
spiced pepitas 162
spicy chicken meatballs 110
spicy chicken thighs with cucumber
    and cashew salad 28
squid salad, spicy, with cucumber
    and capers 14
steak with cherry tomatoes and
    cannellini beans 66
sticky date cake 233
stir-fries
    beef and noodle, with Asian
        greens 109
    chicken, with peanuts and
        cucumber 100
    pork, with hoisin and greens 124
stock 248
sweet potato fries 87
sweet and sour cabbage 69
sweetcorn blinis 162
sweetcorn chowder 246

T

tahini and tomato topping 13
tarts
    apple and cherry 227
    Portuguese custard 207
    raspberry 190
toast toppings
    gravlax and cream cheese 13
    tahini and tomato 13
toast, French raisin 80
toasts, garlic 133
tofu
    broccolini and tofu sambal 33
    egg noodles with tofu and green
        beans 122
    miso, soba noodle and silken tofu
        broth 34

tomatoes
    baked tomato and mozzarella
        pasta 127
    spicy tomato relish 222
    steak with cherry tomatoes and
        cannellini beans 66
    stewed beans in tomato 236
    tahini and tomato topping 13
    tomato and lentil soup 247
    tomato and sumac salad 96
tuna daube 102
tuna salad, white bean, lemon and
    51
turkey, rolled breast, with pistachio
    and cranberry stuffing 224

V

vanilla
    sweet vanilla ricotta 36
    vanilla rice porridge with
        caramelized bananas 42
veal cutlets with shallots,
    mushrooms and balsamic 136
vegetable stock 248

W

walnut pesto 62
watercress, apple and witlof salad
    133
watermelon vodka 163
white bean and chorizo soup 242
white bean, tuna and lemon salad
    51
whiting, crisp, with tomato and
    sumac salad 96

Y

yoghurt
    cucumber and yoghurt relish 237
    cumin, mint and coriander
        yoghurt 140
    herbed 158
    pavlova with yoghurt cream and
        strawberries 176

Z

zucchini fritters with mint 161

ACKNOWLEDGEMENTS

THIS BOOK WOULD NOT HAVE BEEN POSSIBLE WITHOUT THE COMBINED EFFORTS OF MANY DEDICATED AND HARDWORKING INDIVIDUALS.

I'd like to thank Matt Handbury and Juliet Rogers for their commitment to me and my books; Kay Scarlett for her unfailing support and efforts in developing our fourth book together; Jane Price for her seamless and occasionally ruthless editing; Richard Ferretti, who has captured the spirit of Bill Granger and summed it up in a sophisticated package; Lauren Camilleri for creating simple elegant pages; Petrina Tinslay, who once again has outdone herself with superlative photographs; Rebecca Cohen, whose drive, commitment and energy is truly mind-blowing and absolutely inspired (thanks for the home-decorating tips and thank Katie!); Chrissy Freer for her rigorous testing and faultless food; the whole team at bills who work tirelessly; Vanessa Elliott, the driving force behind it all; Neale Whitaker for his patience, leadership and support; Alison Deboo for keeping me and my recipes organized; and finally my family, who, when I can't face cooking another meal, get me back into the kitchen and remind me exactly why I do what I do, and are the best dinner companions imaginable — even if most of the food ends up on the floor!

FOR NATALIE, EDIE, INES AND BUNNY

Published by Murdoch Books Pty Limited.

Murdoch Books Pty Limited Australia
Pier 8/9, 23 Hickson Road, Millers Point NSW 2000
Phone: +61 (0)2 8220 2000 Fax: +61 (0)2 8220 2558

Murdoch Books UK Limited
Erico House, 6th Floor, 93–99 Upper Richmond Road
Putney, London SW15 2TG
Phone: +44 (0)20 8785 5995 Fax: +44 (0)20 8785 5985

Chief Executive: Juliet Rogers
Publisher: Kay Scarlett

Photographer: Petrina Tinslay
Design Concept and Art Direction: Richard Ferretti, Erika Oliveira
Styling and Photographic Art Direction: Rebecca Cohen
Food Editor and Food Styling: Chrissy Freer
Food Assistant: Andrew De Sousa
Editor: Jane Price
Designer: Lauren Camilleri
Production: Megan Alsop

FOR BILL GRANGER:
Executive Producer: Natalie Elliott; Executive Creative Director: Neale Whitaker
Recipe Coordination: Alison Deboo

The publisher, Bill Granger and the creative team would like to thank the following for their generosity in supplying furniture, props, appliances and kitchenware for this book: Accoutrement; Bisanna Tiles; Caesarstone; Chee Soon & Fitzgerald; Cloth; Le Creuset; De De Ce Furniture; Dinosaur Designs; Domayne; Funkis; Furitechnics; Granite & Marble Works; Husmann Communications for the BBQ; Herbies; HWI Homewares; Jarass; Ken Neale 20th Century; Kitchenaid; Les Olivades; Levesons; Miele; Mud Australia; Papaya; Poliform; Publisher Textiles; Simon Johnson; Skipping Girl; The Country Trader; Universal Enterprises; Until; Wild Sets; Hair, make-up and grooming by Ziggy Golden

National Library of Australia Cataloguing-in-Publication Data
Granger, Bill, 1969- .   Every Day. Includes index. ISBN 978 1 74045 858 0.
1. Cookery. I. Title. 641.5

CONVERSION GUIDE: You may find cooking times vary depending on the oven you are using. For fan-forced ovens, as a general rule, set the oven temperature to 20°C (35°F) lower than indicated in the recipe. We have used 20 ml (4 teaspoon) tablespoon measures. If you are using a 15 ml (3 teaspoon) tablespoon, for most recipes the difference will not be noticeable. However, for recipes using baking powder, gelatine, bicarbonate of soda (baking soda) or small amounts of cornflour (cornstarch), add an extra teaspoon for each tablespoon specified. We have used 59 g (2 oz) eggs.